BUILDING A GREAT MARRIAGE

In appreciation for your gift to Focus on the Family, please accept this copy of *Building A Great Marriage* by Anne Ortlund. Your contributions enable Dr. James Dobson and his staff to address the needs of millions of homes in North America today.

We trust that you'll find insights to strengthen and invigorate your marriage in the following pages. We're confident that this book will make a fine addition to your family's bookshelf.

Focus on the Family
P.O. Box 500
Arcadia, CA 91006

By Anne Ortlund

Children Are Wet Cement
Building a Great Marriage
Up With Worship
Disciplines of the Beautiful Woman
Discipling One Another
The Best Half of Life (With Ray Ortlund)
The Acts of Joanna

Building a Great Marriage

Anne Ortlund

Fleming H. Revell Company
Old Tappan, New Jersey

Library of Congress Cataloging in Publication Data

Ortlund, Anne.
  Building a great marriage.

  Bibliography: p.
  1. Marriage—Religious aspects—Christianity.
2. Family—Religious life. I. Title.
BV835.O77 1985   248.4   84-16078
ISBN 0-8007-1239-0

To the memory of
my parents
Brigadier General and Mrs. Joseph Burton Sweet,
United States Army
— Joe and Betty —
who modeled for their family a great marriage

Contents

Preface

I want to catch you quick with this book, while your marriage is still in the start-up phase. *The right things have to happen, to bring you to greatness later.*

You can learn to "think two," and keep outside relationships from messing up your love.

You can learn to spend *under your budget,* and avoid the tensions that get your friends screaming at each other.

You can learn to ask over and over one question—the question that melts away hostility and brings you to your knees together in peace and servanthood.

You can learn to convert unrealistic expectations into *motivating* expectations.

You can do more than avoid divorce (there are more divorces in the first year of marriage alone than in any other); you can learn to build a *great* marriage, on the Gibraltar-rock foundation of the Lord Jesus Christ—*if you use the right building blocks.* I'd like to set those blocks in front of you.

When Ray and I started out in marriage thirty-eight

years ago, we just stumbled our way along, because we didn't know how to tell what was important and what wasn't. We couldn't tell if any of our mistakes and failures were permanently damaging, or which of the things we did were so right they were terrific.

But along with a thousand quarrels and misunderstandings and goofs, we were doing a lot of things right! Gradually our marriage has gone from "good" to "great," and now we can see the process that made it happen. The building blocks are in place. We're solidly fulfilled in God, each other, our work, and our kids. We're saying, "Hey! We're down the road, and our love is hotter than ever!"

I want to show you that process. My dream is that this book will help you to a long, warm, close relationship.

I want to show you the areas of marriage where you can have plenty of room to move around, be creative, kick up your heels, and make a marriage not like anyone else's.

But I also want to show you solid techniques for the danger zones where you don't dare experiment. These are areas where a lot of couples fail.

I told you my dream; I think *your dream is for a truly great marriage,* with all those same fulfillments—in the Lord, in each other, in your work, and probably in children.

What are the building blocks that will build it for you? Let's take a look together.

Building a Great Marriage

1
You're Married!

Marriage is a mistake every man should make.

GEORGE JESSEL

You're really married. You've volunteered to tackle the sweetest, hardest, most wonderful, most exasperating, most terrifying, most ennobling, most difficult, most rewarding and exhilarating job of your life.

A couple of old girl friends ran into each other, and one said, "Hey, Susie, I hear you're married now. How is it?"

Susie said, "I don't like it."

The friend said, "You don't like it? Why not? What's the matter?"

Susie said, "Well, you gotta cook and do the dishes and make the bed—and three weeks later you gotta do the same things all over again!"

You laugh—but are you saying, "I don't like it"?

A wedding is a little like sitting down in a roller coaster. You're full of delighted expectation and suddenly, *vroom!* You've taken off, "for better or for worse," and is it better or worse? Should you laugh—or should you cry "whiplash"?

Dr. Donald Grey Barnhouse, a longtime widower, wrote a note to himself a month before his second marriage:

> My boy, you have hit the JACKPOT, and you are in the position of a man who never had any money and is suddenly coming into a brace of oilwells. Or of a spinster who has just inherited her sister's nine children. Or of a bull who is taking title to a china shop.[1]

I heard someone say recently, "Marriage is a great adventure, isn't it?—like going off to war. . . ."

It's terrific and it's also tough.

Both.

All at once.

The Bible says in First Corinthians 7 that:

1. From now on your body isn't yours anymore. It belongs to your partner, too, so you're to give him/her sex at any time. Only exception: during periods for prayer (verses 1–7).

2. Married couples must not separate or divorce (verses 10,11).

3. Christians married to non-Christians mustn't divorce, either, unless the non-Christian insists (verses 12–16).

4. A single Christian can concentrate on how to please the Lord, but a married one has a double job: how to please the Lord and how to please his/her spouse (verses 32–34).

Understand, then, early marrieds, what you did when you took a partner: *you just permanently complicated your life.* You stepped into something you can never totally undo.

Dr. Rudolph Dreikurs, Professor of Psychology at Chicago Medical School, wrote this: "Marriage does not solve any problem; it is a problem in itself which has to be solved."

So! *You're beginning to face the greatest challenge of your entire life—the challenge to fit together two basically selfish people for maybe fifty or seventy-five years.*

You're challenged to do it through the shock of unpleasant discoveries about each other,

To fit together when you're tired,

When you've run out of money,

When you're sick,

When you have too much to do,

When your parents and friends say to do one thing and your spouse says to do another,

When *your heart* says to do one thing and your spouse says do another,

When *the Lord* says to do one thing and your spouse says to do another,

When you don't know where to turn for comfort or advice. . . .

Through all this and far more, you're challenged to fit together.

Are you scared? Does the future look too full of obstacles, and you'd like to run? Well, let me give you a piece of advice: *don't pressure yourself out of marriage.* Remember, millions of others are married, too, and many of them fulfilled, enjoying God's will, and deeply in love—like me.

Marriage works for those who have the will to work for it. Marriage gives to those who give to it; a great one will cost you plenty. Be prepared to make huge, sometimes unfairly huge, contributions into the common pot of your marriage—freely, generously, joyously, continually—and never measuring what your partner puts in.

"As long as you both shall live," said your vow. You didn't promise *always to feel in love* with your mate. You couldn't promise that, any more than you could promise always to feel happy, or feel at peace, or feel anything. All you promised was to be married. *For life.*

And *on the other side of self-control, sacrifice, even hardship, is greatness.*

So easy does it.

Laugh a lot.

Touch continually.

Keep hope kindled.

Look right into each other's eyes.

Hang in there.
Keep making love.
Stay with Jesus.
Learn the rules. (Hopefully this book will help.)

You're married. Hear it again: you've volunteered to tackle the sweetest, hardest, most wonderful, most exasperating, most terrifying, most ennobling, most difficult, most rewarding and exhilarating job of your life.

Pick those building blocks carefully.

2
Your Expectations and What Should Happen to Them

You may be first-time marrieds or you may be repeat marrieds, but if you're under forty you're probably, in at least one respect, like my friend Linda Murray.

Linda, in a weekly small group with me, had been going with her boyfriend Scott for over a year. They were both solid Christians, both college graduates, both thirty-one, both attractive, and obviously attracted to each other. They were in the same church, had all mutual friends, and their parents and their friends all hoped they'd hurry up and marry.

So you know how my heart sank when Linda told our group she was going to break up with Scott.

She explained to us, "I said something really funny the other night, and he didn't get it at all. I mean, he didn't laugh, he didn't even smile, he just sat there. I'm thinking, if Scott isn't on the wavelength of my humor, maybe he just isn't the right one for me."

"Linda," I said, "your expectations for marriage are so high, they're crazy. Let Scott be a real human being. Give him a break!"

I thought about the "expectations" thing later on, and I thought it might be why a lot of singles are afraid to marry—their picture of marriage is so idealized—and why a lot of marrieds are disappointed.

Linda was typical of her generation (maybe like you). She'd been lectured and "seminar'd" into a picture of marriage in which a Christian man and woman, forever desperately in love, play house in their adorable little completely furnished and equipped apartment, where he strives in every way to "meet her needs," and where she always looks totally happy, sexy, and cherished. Being a symbol of Christ, the husband is always both strong and tender, arriving home from work as fresh as when he left, ready to embrace her with one hand and hold a Bible in the other. That is, unless he's racing joyously to beat her to the dish towel.

The wife, on the other hand, is sharp enough to hold down a good job, but she gets home before he does, so that she can be ready at the door to fall into his arms, and over her shoulder he surveys a shining, polished house, and he smells the aroma of dinner ready to be enjoyed—unless, of course, she should playfully steer him first into the bedroom.

Bills somehow stay paid. Trash never accumulates.

Nobody ever vomits. Nobody ever even burps or has bad breath, or passes gas. When they smile, they never have spinach caught between their teeth. And there's always time on the spur of the moment to throw a picnic into a basket (with checked cloth and a flower), and hand in hand, race to a grassy meadow, where they cuddle so much they forget to eat.

After the honeymoon, the first surprise to any married couple can be how *differently* things turn out (did it surprise you?)—and how *different* the two of you are. Of course you're still in love—but how could your partner be so *different* from what you envisioned, beyond all reasonable expectations?

Toni was blow drying my hair at the beauty salon.

"The first week I was married," she said, "I thought, *What did I do this for? It was better at Mom's!*"

You had hints of your differences over the two ways you viewed your wedding. Most girls want to *get* married; most guys just want to *be* married. (GROOM: "Let's get this wedding over with and get on to the real thing!" BRIDE: "This *is* the real thing!")

But into the first weeks or months of marriage, Prince Charming falls off his horse. And Cinderella didn't fit her slipper after all; you just thought she did. And when the things you dreamed of don't materialize, surprise may turn to disappointment. . . .

Disappointment to disillusionment. . . .

Disillusionment to criticism and quarrels,

And finally to bitterness and estrangement.

Expectations—they can be a trap!

I saw a television show recently that told the story of young divorce. At one point the husband was talking to an older man who'd been married thirty-five years.

"Fred," he said, "how have you and Mary weathered all the years? How have you stayed married, and happily married?"

"Well," mused Fred, "I don't know. I guess back when we got married we didn't expect as much—and so somehow we got more than we expected."

If you are remarried, you probably tended to expect that this time around your mate would be everything the other mate wasn't. But if you're first-time married, the problem's probably worse. In a sense, you can't help it that you weren't born thirty-five years earlier like Fred. Or like me.

(Oh, oh, I feel myself slipping into, "Now, when *I* was young . . . !")

There was no adolescent culture when I started out. We teenagers had no money of our own, so the business world never played up to us. We had little status, so we were eager to grow up and hold jobs and get married, so we could get some! And the "work ethic" was still heavy upon us.

The adolescent culture of today is a play culture, with surf bums, ski bums, and other bums, and the whole movie-music-magazine feed-in encourages a Peter Pan mentality: "I'll never grow up!" "Let me be old enough to drive, drink, travel, marry, and be independent of my parents' and teachers' telling me what to do.

"But when I'm old I don't want to be *old.* I want to remain youthful, playful, fun, free of squares, and making lots of money at a job that doesn't require much of me, so my spouse and I can go on being surf bums and ski bums—together."

Then when life doesn't turn out that way, couples turn on each other; it must have been the other's fault; things would be great if only he/she. . . . I made a mistake, I got the wrong partner, let me out, next time I'll catch the right bus. . . .

They expected too much from each other, much too much—more than any human could deliver.

Here's my suggestion, and *this is going to be the basis for all your building blocks on the way to a great marriage:*

Don't abandon your expectations. (The solution isn't to expect little or nothing; you'd get bored in a hurry.) Don't abandon your expectations—*shift them.*

On what can you really rely? What would you say is so rock-safe that you could expect the moon from it and never be disappointed?

Aha! You've got it! *God Himself, in Jesus Christ, is the only secure, safe foundation for a great marriage.*

You want stars in your eyes. You want great dreams together. All right, *ask Him* for all the good things you want from your marriage.

Said Jesus,

"Everyone who hears these words of mine and does not put them into practice is like a foolish man who builds his house on sand [your own human expectations and efforts].

"The rain came down [financial pressures],

"The streams rose [interfering in-laws],

"And the winds blew and beat against that house [sickness, unexpected pregnancy, loss of job],

"And it fell with a great crash."

Matthew 7:26,27

On the other hand,

"Everyone who hears these words of mine and puts them into practice is like a wise man who built his house on the rock [your expectations in Jesus Christ, your hope in Him];

"The rain came down [financial pressures],

"The streams rose [interfering in-laws],

"And the winds blew and beat against that house [sickness, unexpected pregnancy, loss of job],

"Yet it did not fall, because it had its foundation on the rock."

Matthew 7:24,25

You're starting together to build your house, these early years. *Build it,* the two of you, *on Him.* Search your hearts, separately and together, and make sure that He is now your Savior from sin, your personal Lord, your Shield, your Helper. Seek to found your married life on Him. *The same storms hit every house. Make sure of your foundation.*

Expect less from the marriage in itself. What's marriage? It's like a house—along our California coast, sometimes they slide right into the sea.

Expect more from God! He's the One who can make you a great marriage—solid, secure, enduring, lively, contributing, fun—and a great romance, the joy of everyone who looks at it.

That's the foundation, and you absolutely have to start there, with Him. If you're reading this together, why don't you also read Matthew 7:13–27, and then take hands and ask Him to be your Foundation? . . .

Now you're ready to see what the right building blocks are, and how to lay them.

3

How to Act Like a Husband; How to Act Like a Wife

Marriage is the deep, deep peace of the double bed after the hurly-burly of the chaise lounge.

MRS. PATRICK CAMPBELL

It's terrific, isn't it? You finally have each other. (Ray and I joined each other in Washington, D.C., on a Thursday for our Saturday wedding, and I remember how we hugged and said, "No more separations! From now on we're together!")

And whatever you want to do to love each other—in bed or out—it's *legal.* Halleluia!

Honeymoon times are often euphoric. You'd been counting the days so long, and now it's *here.* You're "Mr.

and Mrs." (We honeymooned in April in Virginia amid spring flowers and dogwood, and we kept saying, "Why do people keep asking us if we're honeymooners? How can they tell?")

Then you settle into your first address, typically a little apartment. *Now* what do you do?

Instinctively "he" starts doing what he saw his dad do, and "she" starts doing what she saw her mother do. Problem: *his dad* never lived with *her mother*.

Robert O. Blood says, "The acid test of role compatibility comes in the first year. . . . Each partner . . . begins acting out his own preconceptions."[2]

In the old days couples knew who they were and what they did. ("I'm a husband. I clear forests and I farm and I shoot game. . . ." "I'm a wife. I clean, I cook. . . .") The children knew clearly what grown-up boys do and what grown-up girls do.

Think of the job a new husband shouldered back then. He was volunteering to administrate a family unit that would have at least six functions:

1. *Productive,* making the furniture, clothing, maybe even the house. Now all that's been taken over by industry.

2. *Protective.* This function is now handled by the police.

3. *Educative.* The schools have assumed this one.

4. *Recreative.* Taken over by movies, TV, and public functions and places.

5. *Religious.* This has been transferred to the church, often completely, or ignored altogether.

6. *Affectional.* This is the area of lovemaking, baby making, and child raising, and it's really the only function left delegated just about entirely to the home.

No wonder guys today feel they have less challenge and less status! And probably both partners work outside the home, and both wear pants, and they cut their hair about the same length, and maybe soon the kids will be saying, "Hello, Mom . . . uh, I mean, Dad. . . ."

And no wonder husbands want to work their way up the "corporate ladder"; they're looking for something to challenge that male longing for importance and purpose and meaning—but oops, there's a spike heel on that rung above them!

Ray and I were out to dinner last night with Dave and Phyllis and Lee and Fran, two godly, thoughtful couples, and we talked about this.

"What does the Bible say a husband should do and a wife should do?" we asked. "Does it say the husband's to be out working and the wife's to stay home with the kids, or is that middle-class tradition?" We thought of the Proverbs 31 woman with both family and businesses. We talked of Lydia, a textile merchant, and Priscilla, making tents with her husband. But we thought how Deuteronomy 6 says to talk about the Lord to your children all the time and in every home situation. That seemed to say that if you have children, at least one parent, apparently either one, ought to be at home with them.

What do you do from Day One of your marriage, to act like a husband, to act like a wife, that's so basic from God's viewpoint that you'll be laying your first block to build a great marriage?

Here's the husband's building block: husband. You say I'm not being clear? Well, change the word "husband" from a noun to a verb. It's something you're to *do,* and very few husbands know this. God asks you to *husband your wife.* What does that mean?

Look at John 15:1 in the King James Version, and Jesus says God's a "husbandman." Look at it in a newer version and it says He's a "gardener." The word's the same, and to "husband" your wife means to seek to tend her as God tends us—to look over her, take care of her, remove from her anything that shouldn't be there, nurture her, and keep her productive and thriving and beautiful.

Husband, she's not your mother—she's your wife, for you to husband. Expect to be able to pick out your own clothes, fry an egg, keep track of where your library card is, and put on your raincoat without being told.

Don't hide behind her skirts. If a magazine salesman comes to the door and you don't want any, don't say, "If it were up to me I'd take them, but I know my wife would say no." Or if it's not a first marriage and you have children, don't always say, "Go ask your mother." Don't lay that on her, now or later. Be a man; stand between her and the hard knocks. *Husband* her.

I see now, looking back, how from the first Ray looked after me, often asked how I felt, made sure I got enough sleep, assumed financial responsibility for me and *cared for me,* like a gardener with his garden. And because I'm not always easy to "husband," over the years Ray learned diplomacy and skill when he saw a weed to pull! He was building the two of us toward a great marriage. And his development in husbanding me prepared him for tending increasingly larger groups of others, until he became a true leader of people.

To husband your wife will challenge you all your life. It will be God's way to "grow you up" and make you *male* in the finest sense.

Here's the wife's first building block: Ephesians 5:33 in the Amplified Version; you're gonna love it!

... and let the wife see that she respects and reverences her husband—that she notices him, regards him, honors him, prefers him, venerates and esteems him; and that she defers to him, praises him, and loves and admires him exceedingly.

Wife, put that over your mirror, read it, memorize it, say it and do it day after day. Why is God's command for the women so key? Because He has made a man's ego unique, precious, and crucial to his "making it" in life.

Dr. Paul Popenoe calls it "a man's dearest, sometimes almost his sole possession."[3]

A wife must understand this to build a great marriage. If she expects financial support (that's part of husbanding), then she must give emotional support. One's as necessary as the other. Just as the husband's to contribute paychecks month by month, she's to contribute admiration and encouragement to her man day by day.

What did you first love about him? Why did you marry him? From the wedding day on, focus on these things and add to them. Don't ever let your affirmations lag.

Dr. Blood interviewed sixty newlyweds for their complaints and found they complained about not enough sexual intercourse; the home not well cared for; ideas not shared, income not properly spent, and other resentments; but the *chief of all complaints was "not enough verbal expression of affection,"* [4] and the husbands complained even more than the wives! Men are often starved for this.

Wife, right now make a little private list of seven things you love about your husband. Then tell him one of those each day for the next week.

That's a start—but both of you must work at it and learn to affirm over and over.

"I love the way your hair curls over your ears!"

"I looked around the room tonight, and there wasn't anybody there as cute as you."

"I'm so proud of you!"

"You're so wonderful!"

And over and over those three magic words, "I love

you." My mother's advice to Ray and me was to say "I love you" at least once every day. We've come pretty close to that.

Husband, *start to act like a husband:* care for and nurture your wife; *husband* her. It will make you truly male.

Wife, *start to act like a wife:* defer to him and praise him. It will make you truly feminine.

These are essential. Together they make a solid building block toward a great marriage.

4

Responsibilities: Who Does What?

Who does what? It really doesn't matter. In almost everything it really doesn't. When you pare down the list, wives still are responsible to have the babies, and husbands still have to impregnate them. But what else?

Happy marriages can result when all kinds of traditional responsibilities are turned around. Take our dear friends Larry and Dolly, married twenty-five years.

Larry's a leader, a great, enthusiastic fellow with a big voice. Dolly's a quiet little thing and rather shy. Larry does all the house decorating for Christmas and other seasons. He arranges their flowers. Once he made a neat little battery-operated fountain for the center of their dining table.

Dolly, on the other hand, had a problem a while back with their refrigerator, and she took the whole thing apart and fixed it. Another time she blacktopped the driveway, and she put a retaining wall around the back of their hillside house.

But Larry's the leader! *They each know who they are.* And they function according to their gifts, and it's okay.

My sister's husband, Chuck, during his seminary student days, pastored a church in rural Pennsylvania, where nearly all the men used to mine coal. But the coal ran out, and gradually the men learned to stay home and run their houses and children, while their wives commuted into town to work.

It's all right—*if it's all right between your ears.* If the male can still feel male, he can do about anything. My dad, a general in the U.S. Army, and my mother took along another general one time on a family picnic. I was sitting there having trouble with my knitting, and this two-star general pulled out the wrong stitches for me and fixed the whole thing. But if he hadn't felt very male, he never could have made it to the top of the Army.

If a woman can still feel female—if she can keep that psychological "covering" on her head which makes her know she's a woman in God's scheme of things—she can do almost anything. Recently a woman doctor sobbed in my arms because she wants a husband! Of course she can practice medicine—but she still knows she's a woman.

But Ephesians 5:21 is so important when you're newly married! "Submit to one another"—fit in with, adapt to one another. What does *he* think male responsibilities are? He may have grown up watching his father or other men carry out the trash and mow the lawn. Until he is very secure in his maleness, he'd better do those.

What does *she* think are female responsibilities? Feeling her way at first, she'd better stick to those.

Maybe it would help to know what other couples mostly do. Look on page 38 to see the traditional approach, according to one study:[5]

A few years from now, after the husband has said a million times, "You're so feminine and adorable!" his wife may feel feminine enough to mix the cement for their new house, or who knows what? And later, when he's heard over and over in his ears, "You big, strong, handsome man!" he may feel secure enough in his masculinity to don an apron and unmold the Jell-O. But don't push it.

The point is to agree. Any new manufacturing company has to decide who makes it, who sells it, and who counts the money.

Sit down one evening this month and make a job list. There's cooking, cleaning up, bedmaking, laundry, keeping up the car if any, bill paying, plant watering, shopping, lawn care and snow shoveling, disciplining the kids, if any—what else? Together check off first what each of you *enjoys* doing; then what each of you thinks you *ought* to do, and last divide up the things neither of you likes.

Use that scheme for about a month. Then try switching some jobs. Try everything sooner or later; you may discover gifts you didn't know you had. And however the jobs finally work out when you get into a pattern, it will help if you both know how to do everything passably— for those times when one is sick or away or the outside job situation changes.

HUSBAND-WIFE RESPONSIBILITIES

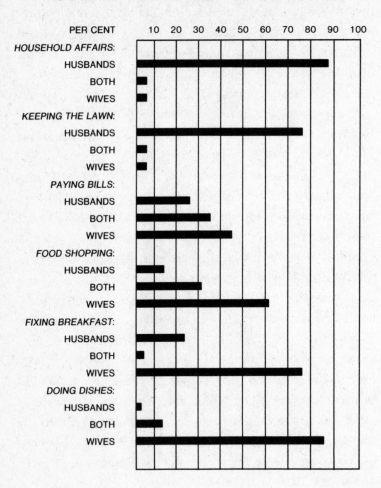

But now about those nagging little details. You're saying, "We know who does the major things. It's the minors that are driving us bananas!"

That's where Romans 15:7 comes in; it says, "Accept one another . . . ." Let me tell you how beautifully that verse fits here.

Every morning I shut Ray's bathroom cupboard door. He never does it; he doesn't notice it; he doesn't even know *I* do it. I could fume and nag at him—but if I'm the one *who cares* that the cupboard door is shut, haven't I already shown that I qualify to shut it? My concern becomes my job. It bugs me to have that cupboard door left standing open; therefore *it meets my need to shut it,* and I cheerfully, even selfishly, consider it my daily task to shut the cupboard door. It keeps me happy!

On the other hand, I would let houseplants grow brittle and stiff in death before I'd give them water. I love our house; I love the colors, shapes, and proportions of the decor, and I understand the spots where a plant needs to be. So if I saw a dead plant there I'd throw it out and go buy another, but it's not in my makeup to think of watering it. Isn't that awful? But Ray accepts me as I am—a helpless, hopeless, plant murderer—and he doesn't scold me. Without a word he just tends to the plants. And that meets *his* need.

(I'd never polish a car, either. Would you believe Ray keeps our cars so meticulously that he even cleans the *underside of the hoods?*)

How do you divide up jobs? Your concerns become your jobs. Enjoy them!

But what if neither one of you cares if the cupboard door hangs open? Let it hang; you can reach the contents faster. What if neither of you cares if the plants stand there dead? Maybe you'd better get plastic. Compatibility is more important.

What if neither of you cares about cooking? Remember the principle: *your concern becomes your job.* Whose tummy growls first? Of course, for fun I've gone to the extreme. A chapter coming soon is going to give you a question to ask which should solve any stalemates.

But learn to *accept one another as Christ accepts you*— scars, warts, lacks, and all—and don't burden each other with expectations and rules.

What do you see that needs doing? Go do it.

5

The Decision-Making
Process That Wins

The real theatre of the sex war is the domestic hearth.

GERMAINE GREER

At first the two of you will probably decide on even the littlest things together. Good. Synchronizing two lives takes lot of togetherness.

"Honey, I've made plenty of beds in my life, and I have *never* put the top sheet on upside down."

"My mother taught me *always* to put it on upside down."

"What's the point?"

"So when you turn it over the top of the blanket it'll be rightside up."

"I've never turned it over the top of the blanket."

"Well, you're supposed to."

"Who says? What great being in the universe made up the unchangeable law that all top sheets must be turned over blankets?"

Before long you'll be treating the top sheet the same way, and over succeeding years it will never be mentioned again; that decision will have become one of the many stuck-together layers of family decisions that gradually form into a nice, strong building block for a great marriage. It's called THE WAY WE DO THINGS AT OUR HOUSE, and it needs to get added to and added to.

Beware of leaving little crumbly bits of things lying around that you can't agree on. They weaken your unity.

"You want to put savings for a bedroom TV in the 'recreation' budget? No way. That's not recreation, that's furniture."

"I know, but it's not important the way a new dresser is. We need a dresser more; you can't treat them alike."

"Look, at the end of a day I need to relax, and a dresser doesn't make me relax. Anyway we've got that old dresser already, but we have no TV in here at all."

"Hey, you promised the new dresser was next! I've been holding off having the girls over to see our place until we get that awful old dresser out of here!"

"Then let's put the living-room TV in the bedroom for now."

"It will leave a big hole in the living room. . . . All right, if we can still get the dresser next."

Good! They came to a new agreement, and that gathered up some messy material of separateness lying around and slapped it onto their building block of THE WAY WE DO THINGS AT OUR HOUSE.

Now, as the time passes you can't decide together every little thing; life gets more complicated. Usually *the one most interested in an area makes decisions about it* ("This gas is making the engine knock, I'll try another brand"; "I'm going to try watering the African violet less.")

That's fine as long as your heart tells you it would be all right with your mate. But understand it means the two of you are building up little separate piles of material which aren't contributing to that building block of family decisions. Try to keep your separate piles down and to keep adding to the block! When you have a little time you might say, "Do you notice this gas is making the engine knock? What do you think, shall I try another brand?" Or, "Do you suppose I'm overwatering this African violet?" You submit to the other's opinion, and something warm happens inside you both.

Well, you can't always find the time to do that, and anyway, as a marriage moves along something insidious happens: you begin to talk to each other less and less. It's a sad fact, but every study indicates the average couple talks together more when they're first married than they ever will again.

As time passes, either in the interest of efficiency or to avoid conflict, husbands and wives initiate little separate piles of their own decisions—little crumbly messes of THE WAY *I* DO THINGS. ("If I asked him/her we might disagree. I already know what I want; I'll do it my way and say nothing.")

And they both neglect to work together on packing hard and tight that precious building block between them.

But it's a crucial block for building a great marriage. And that's what your hearts really long for, don't they? That's why you're reading this book. So why be the average couple? Why not build the hard way, the good way, the right way, and choose to stay warm and close together?

Are you willing? Well, then, we're moving into a danger zone, so put on your hard hats.

When we talk about making decisions together, we're talking about ultimate leadership: somebody to moderate, move things along, and in case of a stalemate, make the final decision.

We'll look at leadership biblically, because this is God's idea, and it will also be practical.

God creates hierarchies. It's true. Believe it. Relax. When He creates something it's got parts and system and order; it fits together. The Bible talks about ". . . his servants, both small and great" (Revelation 19:5). The body of Christ has parts with varying status (1 Corinthians 12:18–25).

In the beginning, God made animals, fish, and birds; then He made people to *rule over* the animals, fish, and birds (Genesis 1:26).

Of the people, first He made a man; then He made a woman to help the man (*see* 2:18). If "help" sounds demeaning to you, the same word is used about God Himself: "He is our help" (Psalms 33:20).

Yes, and 1 Corinthians 11 says that God is the head of Christ, and Christ is the head of man, and man is the head of woman. Does that mean the woman is inferior to the man? Not unless Christ is inferior to God.

Christ and God are equal—even one—yet with different functions. So the man and the woman are equal (Galatians 3:28)—even one (Genesis 2:24)—and yet with different functions.

What are the functions? The husband is to lead, the wife is to follow (Ephesians 5:22–33). *It may be tough,* but they are both asked to submit to those roles! Ephesians 5:21 says that everyone is to submit to everyone.

So how does the husband submit? Whether he is comfortable with leading or not, whether he naturally has the gift of leadership or not—in his own home, in obedience to Christ, *he submits to the Lord's command that he lead*—with all that leadership involves. Gradually he'll learn how!

How does the wife submit? Well, she submits to her husband's leadership out of obedience to Christ who commands it. Maybe in her own personality she's the leader of the two, but gradually she'll learn how to follow, with grace and enthusiasm.

What does male leadership mean? It doesn't mean, "No, we won't buy a newspaper tonight." "I insist we have rice instead of noodles."

And male leadership doesn't mean, "My wife decides on the budget and where we'll take our vacations. But I get to decide the big issues—like what should be the government debt ceiling!"

Harry Truman kept a sign on his presidential desk which read, "The buck stops here." And that's leadership: taking the final responsibility for how the whole thing turns out. Said the Lord about His man Abraham as He designated him "the father of many nations," "For I have chosen him, so that he will direct his children and his household after him to keep the way of the Lord *by doing what is right and just . . .*" (Genesis 18:19, italics mine).

That's an enormous job. It doesn't require being macho and dominating. In fact, soon after this pronouncement of God's about Abraham, God was advising him, ". . . listen to whatever Sarah [your wife] tells you . . ." (21:12).

What does it mean, then, to lead? Ephesians 5 gives specific ways the husband is to be "head of the wife as Christ is the head of the church, his body. . . ." The overall method is *to love her as Christ loved the Church.* Then it tells specifically how Christ loved the Church, and therefore how the husband's to love his wife. Actually it's a more detailed, two-part explanation of what it means to "husband" your wife:

1. *Give yourself up for her,* to make her holy, complete, mature. Christ went all the way to death. Calvary love will endure anything for the sake of helping her become all that God planned for her to be.

2. *Cleanse her with the regular washing of the Word of God.* How specific can Ephesians 5 be? It says one of the

ways you lead her and love her and improve her is to "wash her" with God's Word.

The goal is that you might have a wife to *present to yourself*—a gift to yourself!—who is radiant, without a blemish, holy, and blameless! "A wife of noble character is her husband's crown ..." (Proverbs 12:4); she will "adorn" you; she will enhance your image. And when *she's* dressed in purple, *you'll* be respected in the gates of the city (Proverbs 31:22,23).

Look, in many ways you can't help what she is right now. But thirty years from now she ought to be *just what you've made her!*

All that is down the road—but begin now and do yourself a favor: love her with total, self-sacrificing love, and wash her daily with the purifying water of the Scriptures.

That's male leadership, from God's perspective. That's how you're to be the head of your wife. All the details work out from there.

And what does it mean for the wife to submit to her husband? Back in Genesis 2:18, Eve was created to be, as the King James Version says, "a help *meet*" for Adam (italics mine). Somehow we've confused this with the word "helpmate" and come up with "help-meet."

But "meet" is an adjective, and it means "suitable" or "appropriate." It means God made her just right for Adam, the way you fit pieces of a puzzle together. His strengths compensated for her weaknesses. Her strengths compensated for his weaknesses. Together they made what neither could have been alone.

A while back a woman who'd been voted "Mother of the Year" was being interviewed on television.

Said the MC, "Who's the boss in your home?"

"My husband is," she said quickly.

The MC asked with a snicker, "And who decided that?"

She answered immediately, "I did!" And the audience laughed.

But who else could have? The right kind of submission is always a voluntary thing. It can't be demanded by the husband! In a godly marriage nobody demands rights; that would spoil it all. Each insists on the best for the other, and goes to the utmost lengths to get it.

But the crux of God's plan is the husband's leadership. There is that ultimate point where he's to make final decisions. A two-vote system has the potential for canceling each other out. God's plan for marriage is progress and forward momentum, and He builds in a solution for a possible stalemate. The husband listens to her viewpoint with the most earnest, sensitive consideration, but then there's that lonely place of his own "Oval Office."

Sometimes he'll make mistakes; that's the pain of being president. Sometimes she'll know with all her heart that he's wrong; that's the pain of being vice-president.

The story is told that when Ronald Reagan became President of the United States, there was a group of men around him who said, "Mr. President, our lives are dedicated to making you the very best president you can possibly be." And that should also be the heart of a godly wife!

But the offices must be left as God intended them. If the relationship really does picture Christ and His Church, then the wife can no more say, "I refuse to submit to my husband" than the Church can say, "I refuse to follow Christ"! And the husband can no more say, "I refuse to lead my wife" than Christ can say, "I refuse to be Head of My Church"! Only God's plan works out really well.

Blood and Wolfe's sample testing shows that the most unhappy wives are not "the unconsulted wives of dominant husbands, but 'deserted' wives left with the burden of making decisions" alone. Here's the way the chart comes out:

A. When she is dominant, her satisfaction score is only 4.40 (Blood and Wolfe's way of marking). She's unhappy.

B. When he is dominant it's a little higher: 4.64. At least that's better.

C. When they make decisions separately it's 4.70. She's getting her own way, and yet she's just a shade happier than when he's dominant.

D. But when they make decisions together it's 5.06. She likes that best of all.[6]

D, then, is the norm for keeping a happy wife, with *B* for emergency situations!

Go back and back to each other for consultation. "How shall we do this?" "What do you think about that?" Stay close. Talk. Build well your block of THE WAY WE DO THINGS AT OUR HOUSE.

6

Start to "Think Two"

When my husband won a trip for two to Hawaii, he went twice.

The prevailing spirit of our New Day is the spirit of "thinking one." This is the spirit that says,

"I love me, all by myself.

"I love massage parlors, beauty parlors, 'fat farms'—any place that serves me and touches me for my pleasure or improvement but requires nothing of me emotionally.

"I love to dance without touching at all. I like aerobics and jogging, the improvement of 'me' without touching.

"I am unhealthily obsessed with my own health. I love diets and vitamins and health foods. Oh, and desserts.

"I love to think about my self—my weight, my colors, my gifts, my personality. Test me. Let's talk *me*.

"I will make my own way in my career. Whatever happens to the others, I want to come out on top.

"Some of the songs of my generation reflect my mood: 'I Did It My Way,' 'Free to Be Me'. . . ."

Sometimes "thinking one" goes further:

"Birth prevention and abortion keep me free.

"I'm a 'consenting adult' to drugs, alcohol, and sex, my own private pleasures.

"My picture of marriage is jogging down the road of life side by side, free to pursue separate careers and each do our own thing. Maybe we'll meet for lunch."

The philosophy behind "thinking one" is, "I'm on the throne; I'm out for me first. Above all, I want independence. I must be free to be my own person, to pursue what I want, to develop myself, to take care of my own needs first—I must even be free to cut myself loose from anyone, spouse or otherwise, who hinders *me.*"

Self has become our newest idol, maybe our final one: Second Timothy 3:2 says that in the last days "people will be lovers of themselves."

Now, picture it: two independent singles come together in marriage. Can they each import into the new situation their separate feelings of "thinking one," and expect those two entities to feel cozy together?

No way! Those two entities will *fight.* "Don't upset my patterns. Don't challenge me. Don't cross my will! I'll back off; I'll protect myself from you. Don't try to mess with me! If you do, I'll bolt. . . ."

Listen a minute. Be quiet, calm down. Listen to these words carefully: *what are you afraid of?*

A famous European psychiatrist was asked what he

considered one single key word for marriage. His answer: *"Surrender."*

Relax. Lay down your arms. Die a little inside. Hear the Lord Jesus, approaching the cross, say,

> "The man who loves his life will lose it, while the man who hates his life in this world will keep it for eternal life."
>
> John 12:25

In the long run, it's how you win it all!

"Thinking one" never sees the needs and the glory of something bigger: *our* marriage, *our* alma mater, *our* church, *our* neighborhood, *our* country, *our* world—the larger groupings for which we sacrifice something within ourselves, and in sacrificing, find wholeness and fulfillment as individuals.

It's too late to "think one"; you're married! Merge. Blend. "Think two." You're now half of a pair. You must learn to lean on, to trust, to need, to be incomplete without, to long for each other, if a great marriage is to be built for you.

It took Ray and me years to merge, and when it happened, it happened suddenly, but it became a building block. We were studying to teach Ephesians 5 together, and we mused over verse 31, ". . . the two will become one flesh."

"Ray," I teased, tweaking his nose, "that's my nose." I grabbed his arm: "And that's my arm; I've got four arms."

I think he thought I was a little weird, and yet from that study on, sometimes he called me not "Anne" but "my other self." And I would say to him, "When I thought of you as someone apart from me, that guy over there, I could fight you and compete with you and try to hurt you. But if you're *me,* I want to be good to *me!*"

This building block has a double layer. The inner part is the *scriptural doctrine* of being married according to Ephesians 5, of merging from "two ones" to "one two." Then the outer layer is your continual obedience to that, *reshaping your mind-set to conform to that truth.*

Whenever you can, say "we" instead of "I." "We don't go out on Thursday nights." "We love frozen yoghurt."

Introduce yourselves with your last name; start a new trend. First names separate you; your last name combines you. Not "I'm John." "I'm Sally." But "We're the Smiths—John and Sally Smith." Plant it in people's minds, and you'll plant it in your own. According to Cooley's principle of the looking-glass self, after a while you'll feel more "two." You'll *feel married.*

Establish traditions as soon as you can; family rituals are binding. Always wash your hair and polish your shoes together on Saturday nights. Or always read the Sunday paper all the way through on Sunday afternoons. Or always have chili for supper Sunday nights. Do special things on holidays that are just what *you two* do to celebrate.

Do you share a favorite color? Dress up your apartment with it. Is there a table game you both like to play?

Make it a once-a-week thing, a certain night you save for that—with cookies and milk, or veggies and dip, or something that celebrates "We are us!"

My writing was interrupted just now. Nels called upstairs, "Mom, telephone for you! Someone named Jed Freeman."

Jed Freeman . . .? Jed Freeman had been my boyfriend from age fourteen to twenty. He was headed for med school, after which we would go to the mission field. Then when we were college juniors Jed decided he didn't want to be a missionary, and we parted company.

Boy, when I write that it sounds so easy! It was one of my few truly painful moments, when I wrote to Jed to say that because I felt God's will for my life included being open to missions, we were breaking up. That was forty years ago. . . .

"Hello."

"Anne, this is Jed Freeman."

"I don't believe it. Really? *Imagine!* Where are you, Jed?"

"I'm right here in Corona del Mar." He gave the cross streets.

"Can you come see me, Jed?"

"If you have time."

In five minutes he was here. I tried to look deep into his eyes, to see the boy I had known in this mature face. He was there, and the chuckle was the same.

We've spent the last couple of hours talking, remem-

bering, catching up, looking around the house, and driving to our Renewal Ministries office, where he and Ray
met each other for the first time.

He's gone again, and I've come back to my writing,
thinking about the effect Jed has had on my life. Going
with a boy six years, your lives get very intertwined. You
build up a lot of memories. There's a lot to get *disengaged*
from, to give yourself away to somebody else—to feel
married, to "think two."

He's there in the shadows of your mind. When your
marriage is good, his image dims, but at other times. . . .

You compare how *he* would have reacted in a situation, and it's always better.

You think about what *would have been,* if you'd married him instead.

You daydream about his sudden return: he's still in
love with you, and he can't stand it any longer. . . .

If I am typical, even with almost two years between my
breakup with Jed and my marriage to Ray, it was another
few years before his image didn't haunt me. With *three
babies* I was still remembering *Jed* . . . ?

That's crazy. That's counterproductive. It tells me Ray
had to wade through a lot of stuff in my head (thankfully
unknown to him), before he had my full attention. I'm
sure that slowed down our process of fusing well.

Nobody had told me to *"feel married,"* to *"think two,"*
to deliberately dismiss third parties from the corners of
my mind. It would have forged a great marriage a lot
faster.

I have a feeling someone's reading this whose thoughts

have already been roving. My friend, is this a problem with you?

Stop reading for a minute. Commit this to the Holy Spirit, and let Him flood your mind. He understands. He's a Person, but He's not a single. He is merged into a perfect unity with the Father and the Son, and none complete without the others.

Be fully, totally married in your minds. Then every experience of "two-ness" will secure you as a couple more and more:

When one of you loses your job, *think two.* Groan together, and express your love and faith.

When someone flirts with you, *think two,* and tell him/her to bug off.

When your partner shares a secret with you, *think two,* and keep your confidence against all the outside world.

When someone criticizes your partner to you, *think two,* and defend him/her.

Never play down your mate to someone else—not to your mother or your best friend. Be loyal, no matter what. *Think two!*

Fuse. Merge. There was a dreamy old song that expressed it:

> You've got to give a little, take a little,
> And let your own heart break a little—
>   That's the story of,
>   that's the glory of love. . . .
>   You've got to win a little, lose a little,
> And always have the blues a little—

> That's the story of,
>   that's the glory of love.[6a]

Early marrieds, choose for yourselves a new mind-set. Choose to *think two*.

Until you're thinking a brand-new, Ephesians 5:32 kind of *one!*

7

The Question That Can Turn a Good Marriage Into a Great One

Marriage is like taking a bath. After you've been in it a while, it's not so hot.

You feel within you dreams and potential and undeveloped gifts, and you live in a world which encourages you to feel them. In fact, you live in an age of self-realization and opportunity never known in the world before. And you were feeling so young and free. . . .

Until you married. Of course you love your mate, and you didn't want to grow alone, but you did want to *grow*.

Suddenly you've been thrown into a mold. The men are supposed to earn money, but they're not free anymore to spend it as they want. The wives are supposed to feather some kind of nest; you wouldn't mind if this meant decorating it, but it turns out to mean *cleaning* it (even though you have a job, too, which isn't fair), and he's to help with the decorating, and his tastes are gauche.

Matrimony sounded so wonderful. . . . Now you find it's bristling with *A,* obligations and *B,* restrictions.

Subtly you're both sliding into a mind-set of self-pity and resentment and frustration, which could make you miserable, *unless—*

Unless you learn to put into your marriage this building block: one powerful question.

Ask it over and over. Ask it all the rest of your life. Ask it until you're probably still mumbling it in your sleep. Here's the question which will lift you from resentment to joy:

"WHAT CAN I DO TO MAKE YOU HAPPY?"

Stop right now and repeat this question slowly in your mind, several times.

Now let's break the question apart.

1. *"WHAT?"* There are no restrictions here, no limitations to your life-style. You're free from "the law," the cultural overlay of society's expectations. You're free from the "traditions of men"—doing things just because that's the way people have always done them.

"What" introduces a wide-open range of possibilities of life-style for your unique marriage.

2. "What *CAN I DO?"* This part of the question is just

for you. You're not responsible before God for your mate's actions. It will be wonderful if he/she also learns to ask this question, but remember this: *your peace does not depend on anyone else's behavior.* Ultimately, you'll answer to God alone for what kind of marriage partner *you* become.

Ask Him to open your eyes and give you creativity and wisdom and fun and enlarged horizons on WHAT YOU CAN DO.

3. "What can I do *TO MAKE YOU HAPPY?*"

This gives a brand-new orientation, a shift in focus from you to your partner. It's a monumental order. It will take the rest of your together-days to learn to know your mate so well, that you'll understand how to answer this question.

It's a day-by-day, even moment-by-moment question.

HUSBAND (*to himself*) Right now, what can *I do* to make *her happy?* I'll look into her eyes and tell her what I did at work today. She always seems curious to know.

WIFE (*to herself*) Right now, what can *I do* to make *him happy?* He seems to be bugged when things are messy. I'll put away the laundry real quick, and pick up the bedroom, so when he walks in he'll have a sense of order and peace around him. Bless his heart, I think I married a nester! How neat!

HUSBAND What can *I do* to make *her happy?* She's worked like a dog all day. I'll slide out of my chair, while she's having her last cup of coffee, and get these dishes started.

Oh, the pleasure of it! It's a great, great question, a problem-solving question.

And over the longer haul:

WIFE What can *I do* to make *him happy?* I'm married to a guy who's ambitious at work; I'll ask if he'd like to have his boss over for a nice dinner.

(*Or*) I know he loves intellectual conversations. I'll see how he feels about my taking a night course at college.

(*Or*) He's such a great big guy, and I know it's tough on him to live in this tiny apartment. I won't bug him to fix it up too much, but I'll put away all I can toward a larger place.

She's continually asking herself, "What can *I do* to make *him happy?*" It's a question that releases the role of servanthood—so sweet, so deep, so hard, so wonderful, so rare among us. She's not feeling restricted or tied by obligations; she's *doing what she most wants to do*—make her husband happy.

The "WHAT" gives her freedom to be creative and even choose the timing of her actions. The "WHAT" may include scrubbing the kitchen floor, but she has a result, a goal, in mind: HIS HAPPINESS. And that makes the yoke easy and the burden light.

The "CAN I DO" frees her to think how she can make him happy with her own unique set of skills and gifts. It may include baking a rhubarb pie (mine does, for Ray), or saving for tickets for a ball game, or learning to give a good massage; but it will be a different set of gifts to him than any other wife will give.

HUSBAND (*thinking to himself*) Over the long haul, what can *I do* to make *her happy?* I notice she never seems to get enough "sweet words" from me. I'll set a personal goal of affirming her at least three times a day.
(*Or*) I know she gets turned on by the mountains. I'll ask Steve if his folks' mountain cabin is available this summer, when I could get some time off.
(*Or*) She reads her Bible every bedtime, and she's never said a word about my doing it, too, but I know it would make her happy, so I better give it a shot.

The direct question, with the words "I" and "YOU," and looking right into your partner's eyes, is a terrific relationship strengthener: "Honey, what can I do to make you happy?" It melts away every hostility.

It's maybe the *only* question to ask in lovemaking! Look at it again:

1. *"WHAT?"* Theoretically, the sky's the limit. Read the "Song of Songs" again for some of God's fresh ideas.

2. "What *CAN I DO?"* "Here is my body: my hands, my neck, my genital area, my feet, my back, my legs, my lips. . . . They're all available to you."

3. "What can I do *TO MAKE YOU HAPPY?"* "Have you some restrictions in your mind? Then in those

areas I won't offend you. But what gives you pleasure? Does this? Does that?"

The greatest question for any marriage, to be said over and over "as long as you both shall live": "WHAT CAN *I DO*—TO MAKE *YOU HAPPY?*"

Servanthood, the fitting in with and surrendering to others, may over the years cause some of your gifts and dreams to grow and others to wither away, and it won't have been of your choosing.

You started out married life with those feelings of undeveloped talents and potential, and maybe some seem to lie buried for a long time—maybe forever.

So be it.

Your spirit will have enlarged into greatness. You'll have become the person God meant you to be—a perfect stone on a beach polished and made beautiful by the buffeting action of the surrounding elements.

A "career woman" portrait painter in Canada married a pioneer missionary to China, and went with him into a life which never used her art again. Her name was Rosalind Goforth—immortal for her writings on prayer, as never her fine portraits would have made her immortal.

And how did it come about? She simply fell in love with a wonderful man, and under God's tough but tender leading said to Jonathan Goforth, "WHAT CAN I DO TO MAKE YOU HAPPY?"

8

Make Communication Your Favorite Indoor Sport

A good marriage would be between a blind wife and a deaf husband.

MICHEL DE MONTAIGNE (1533–1592)

Ray and I have always been poor at communicating. One of our first dates was to an organ concert at the college chapel. Navy men couldn't go off campus where I lived, so we agreed to meet at the chapel door. The problem was, a door has two sides. He waited on the inside and I on the outside for twenty minutes.

And ever since, too often his words don't say to me what he means, and vice versa, and we both get into hot water.

We were leaving to speak in a foreign country which doesn't like Christian ministers, and we'd had a hard time getting visas. We applied months in advance, and the consulate granted them the last ten minutes before it closed on the Friday before our Sunday departure! (How to get frayed nerves.)

Sunday afternoon we were shutting up the luggage to leave for the airport.

Ray said, "Do you have our visa?"

"Ray!" I exploded, "keeping those visas wasn't my responsibility! I never had them, I never saw them, and if you don't have them with the passports, we're absolutely sunk!"

"Dear," he said mildly, "I meant our Visa *card*. Do you have our Visa card?"

See what I mean?

Ray and I know about every one of the following situations; how about you?—

> I hurt
>   when you reject me;
> you cry
>   when you don't understand me.
> I give up
>   when you put me down;
> you become frightened
>   when I don't talk.
> I feel inadequate
>   in the light of your expectations;
> you feel hopeless

> when nothing seems to change.
> I feel maimed
>   when you don't answer,
> you are alarmed
>   at my indifference. . . .[7]
>
> ULRICH SCHAFFER

From the beginning of marriage the temptation is not to communicate well. Why is that? Because:

1. You might hurt each other.

2. You might be blamed or criticized.

3. You might be misunderstood—or rejected.

4. You might spoil the wonderful happiness of your relationship.

5. Worst of all, your mate might see you as you really are, and not love you anymore.

These are enormous risks. Why not play "let's pretend" and hope the problem will go away?

It won't. And you're leaving a gaping hole in your marriage where the building block of good communication must go.

It takes courage to communicate. Suppose the wife isn't reaching a climax when you're making love. The world says, "Fake it till you make it." But what do *you* say?

Admit your failure. Humble yourself to say, "Help me,

I need you." This may awaken your husband to greater sensitivity and concern than he would otherwise ever give you. You'll both be communicating!

Paul Tournier wrote in *To Understand Each Other,* "Many couples put aside certain subjects—those that are emotionally charged. . . . Thus bit by bit they are starting to become strangers to one another."[8]

Robert O. Blood says, "Couples who tell each other their troubles [early] . . . rely most often on each other for therapeutic relief [later on]. Those who share more of their personal news with each other early in their relationship are more open with each other in later years. . . . Vital interpersonal relationships grow from year to year; weak ones tend to shrivel."[9]

So the early habits are important.

If your work is difficult you may say, "Please, when I come home I don't want to hash it all over again, I want to forget it and relax." But *your goal is communicating, merging, feeling married, "thinking two"!* Then pulling down the curtain on your partner means that now you've got two problems instead of one.

Take the time to talk. And to listen. Look right into each other's eyes as you do both. The more you give details at first, the more satisfied your mate will become. Later he/she has the general picture; you'll just fill in current details; but he'll feel he's sharing in a major part of your life.

Let me hand you the building block of communication. Turn it over and see the big word imprinted on it. What does it read?

"NOTICE," you say, and you look at me puzzled.

Yes, that's the key word. It's so simple, how do so many married people miss it? This is what will help you start to communicate: *notice your partner.*

Most marrieds don't. When one or both go off to work, neither knows what the other was wearing. When they're both at home, neither could say for sure where the other is—in the bathroom, in the yard? If one looks tired, the other doesn't notice.

' A marriage hurts when you've had a cut finger for a week, and he never saw; you shaved off your mustache to please her, and she never said a thing.

Don't just bustle around, functioning! Start to *notice one another.* It could save your marriage. At best, it could build it toward a great one.

Notice. Get the habit of checking each other's *face* every time you encounter each other, even every few minutes.

And the other's *manner.* Does everything seem okay?

Then *acknowledge that you notice.* Greet your mate every time he/she enters the room, even if he's just gone a few minutes.

When she pours your coffee look in her eyes, smile, and say, "Thank you." When he opens the door for you, do the same.

When he gets a haircut, tell him he looks nice. When she housecleans, tell her everything looks great.

And *keep noticing.* "You look good today, sugar." "Have I seen that hair ribbon before?" "Are you okay?" "You look tired." "What's the grin for?" *Keep noticing.*

In the mornings ask how he slept. In the evenings ask how the day went. "How's your heart?" "How do you feel?" "Are you happy?" "What can I do to make you happy?"

Practice your spouse's "there-ness." Reach over and touch. Let your eyes meet. Blow a kiss. Make a face. Invent a secret signal. It all says, "I see you. I care about you, I appreciate you, *I notice you.*" That's an essential building block.

But in spite of it all, you'll miscue and misunderstand and quarrel, and you'll think you're never going to figure out that stranger you're married to.

I love what Rilke, the German poet, wrote to a friend, that "even between the closest human beings, infinite distances continue to exist," but that "a wonderful living side by side" can develop if they "succeed in *loving the distance between them*" (italics mine).

That's good! Keep the space between you friendly so you assume the best of each other, and then forgiveness will come quickly when it's needed.

The more different your backgrounds and your previous cultures and points of view, the more you'll misunderstand each other. But *understand that you'll misunderstand,* and don't give up.

Let's face it: sin is what makes communication a problem. The "self" in us says, "I'm certainly a reasonable person, and my opinion is basically good, and I stated it as correctly as I know how, so what's the matter with this nerd who can't comprehend simple English?"

A British fellow took a 'round-the-world trip, and he

wrote in his diary, "Yes, indeed, one certainly sees and hears some peculiar things. Take such a simple item as H_2O. In Germany they call it *wasser,* in Spain *agua,* in China *shwai,* and so on. Strange blokes some of those people are. After all, the stuff is *water.*"

Now when you really find out how to communicate well, come tell Ray and me. We're tired of aiming too high or too low and missing each other.

Here's something which might help. Ray and I plan to try it, too:

Five-Step Exercise to Help Communication

Fifteen minutes a day (in the evening, if possible), maybe at the end of dinner together before dishes, one spouse per evening:

1. Write a few sentences on one of the following:

   "This is where I'm coming from. ..."
   "This is who I am. ..."
   "This is what I like to do. ..."
   "This is what I'm thinking these days. ..."
   "This is what I was trying to tell you earlier. ..."
Don't write too long.

2. Read the other what you wrote, out loud.

3. Then the other reads it back to you, out loud, following which,

4. He puts the paper down and repeats the gist of it in his own words.

5. Then she first responds with, "Yes, that's what I meant," or else makes corrections until the other has it right.

Then the next evening it's the other's turn.

P.S. T. S. Matthew said, "Communication is something so simple and difficult that we never can put it in simple words."[9a] Now, isn't that the truth? This is my most worked-over chapter, and I feel as if I just got started.

9
Reconciliation: The Art of Making Up

"There are two sides to every argument, until you take one."[9b]

"Your liberty to swing your arms ends where my nose begins."[10]

Understand from the first that you're going to fight. Hopefully not physically!

I remember when I was small, a little boy the age of my brother Bobby was banging Bobby over the head with his train. Up came a window, and the kid's mother leaned out and called, "Frankie, don't hit that little boy with your train! Use your fists!"

I haven't seen Frankie since, so I don't know how he's doing with a wife.

But even verbal fights are painful, aren't they? Basically it's because of sin that we bicker and clash and harangue. Even having said that, I hope you argue sometimes.

Let me tell you what's worse than arguing. Elizabeth Achtemeier tells about a "fine Christian woman who has driven her husband to drink. She is loving, forgiving, irenic and patient, and she simply drives her husband nuts because *she will not listen seriously to him when he becomes angry.* For this woman, anger and conflict are wrong. Therefore when her husband shouts or rages, she waits out his anger patiently, and then tenderly forgives and forgets everything he has said. The result is that her husband feels he is beating himself against a stone wall."[11]

When you and your partner come together out of two separate backgrounds, you are going to misunderstand each other; you're going to clash. And it's imperative to air your different opinions if you're ever going to get yourselves flowing eventually into one stream.

You wish you could hear each other out without ever raising your voices—but the fact is, you care so much! If a neighbor disagrees with you, you can decide he's crazy and shrug it off. But when your wife or husband disagrees with you, you care terribly.

At this point couples can hate arguing too much and back off into silence and become strangers. *Then their marriage is dying.*

Other couples can avoid painful topics, stick to happy ones, and pretend everything is fine. *Their marriage is dying, too.*

"They dress the wound of my people
     as though it were not serious.

'Peace, peace,' they say,
  when there is no peace."

Jeremiah 6:14

When your partner blows off steam, listen carefully.
Something important is there underneath.

Of course, if this happens all the time, what's important
is that your partner has a temper! Well, *why* does your
partner have a temper? Perhaps there's frustration there
because in the past he/she wasn't taken seriously unless
he shouted.

Ray was the baby of five children and he was like that,
which made him start off married life with a real temper.
Well, when I'd goaded my big brother Bobby through the
years, he didn't make it any big deal. So when I goaded
Ray, I was constantly surprised that he reacted so
strongly.

Once in a sudden temper he turned our car and
rammed it into a snowbank. Then he couldn't back it out
again, and a fellow he'd been witnessing to came along
and helped him get it out, saying, "Gosh, how'd your car
get in *here?*"

Another time he threw an empty coke bottle down on
our dark-stained dining room floor, and the scar was
there from then on. We never could get rid of it.

The temper was *his* sin, but the goading was *mine,* and
only when the *two* of us repented did his temper begin to
wane. Honestly, it rarely shows itself anymore.

Well, how do the two of you get your thinking together? Your slogan could be, "Confrontations yes, arguments no!" That is, be willing to disagree and to probe to understand each other until you come to terms; but try to do it without throwing each other around the room or stomping on each other. Fair enough?

Confrontations will degenerate into arguments—

1. If they last too long.

2. If they go from impersonal to personal, from discussing to insulting.

3. If they move to off-limit areas (handicaps or weaknesses which can't be helped, or sins of the past which need to be forgotten).

4. If they involve non-negotiables—subjects where your partner's thinking is permanently in cement. (Back off and love him/her *as he is.*)

5. If it's the wrong time of day or night, if it's before a meal, if it's when your mate is upset or off balance anyway. Those are yellow-light, maybe red-light times. Get smart in your confrontations!

But sometimes you won't be smart. You're tired, you're down, you say something that's taken wrong—and oh-oh—a storm has broken loose. If you've been communicating well on sunny days (affirming each other, caring for one another), you can ride it out without capsizing.

In our early marriage the storms were painful because we didn't know each other too well yet, confrontations were still unfamiliar to us, and we didn't know how it would all turn out. We couldn't measure how damaging our difference of opinion would be. But Ray was great in the sunny times about courtesies and loving affirmations. So I can remember the very period in our marriage when our relationship was secure enough that when we broke into arguments—when storms came—we already knew the weather forecast: clearing and sunny ahead. We could predict that soon we'd be hugging and apologizing. Actually, sometimes from then on, when we'd argue we'd break out in giggles.

But not always. The more you love, the more differences can hurt.

So get skilled in the art of reconciliation.

What's the key to making up so that the thing is really healed and finished? *Forgiveness,* God's style.

Second Corinthians 5:18–21 is the Bible's classic passage on reconciliation, speaking of God's technique for overcoming His quarrel with mankind. It says that by means of the cross "God was reconciling the world to himself in Christ, *not counting men's sins against them*" (verse 19, italics mine). There it is! He "blotted them out" (*see* Isaiah 43:25), "remembering them no more" (*see* Hebrews 10:17), so that He could begin fresh with us!

And that's what we have to do with each other. There's a personal "cross" involved again, every time sin separates us from each other. "Stated psychologically," writes David Augsburger, "forgiveness takes place when the person who was offended and justly angered by the offender bears his own anger, and lets the other go free."[12]

A man had a whole box full of letters and papers in his safe—the clear evidence of his wife's unfaithfulness to him. They were his ticket to freedom. But God did a new work both in his heart and in hers. For her part, she humbly asked his forgiveness. For his part, he took from the safe the entire box, every letter, every paper, and threw them all into the fireplace, and the two of them watched them all destroyed forever.

Now please don't hurry through this next sentence; it's a whopper.

> The degree to which we are able to forgive others is the degree to which we can be open to the love of Jesus in our lives.[13]

Husband and wife, expect to have to be reconciled to each other over and over and over.

Expect to realize you're drifting apart, you've misunderstood each other again, and make your way back together by conscious effort, time after time after time.

Expect to be hurt, and let "forgiveness, God's style" heal each hurt.

I love you is a strong building block toward a great marriage. *I'm sorry* is an equally strong one.

10
Why Commitment Works

I'm tired of all this nonsense about beauty being only skin deep. That's deep enough. What do you want—an adorable pancreas?

JEAN KERR

When you got married you probably repeated words something like these:

For better, for worse,
For richer, for poorer,
In sickness and in health,
As long as we both shall live.

The lights were soft; the loving eyes of all were upon you; it seemed at that moment a thrilling thing to say.

But now there's the living out of what you said—living out those words for *how many years?* Maybe seventy-five? Doggone! You just shouldn't have carried it that far, right?

If you were to make a list of all the negative things that have happened since you got married—my gosh, just *in this short a time*—what else might be coming up in those almost endless years ahead? So sometimes you're saying to yourself—right?—"Forget it! I didn't ask for this! I'm gonna find me an *exit!*"

Hold it.

You're trapped.

You can't get out—for lots of reasons.

First, you're a person of honor, and *you gave your word.* Forget the statistics and all the marriage breakups around you: *you are different.*

Or you've come out of previous smashed marriages? Well, this is your fresh start; "God is the God of new beginnings." You have Him to help you, and from now on *your word is going to be good.*

"For better, for worse," you said. Maybe *much* worse. He is consumed with ambition; you just wanted a nice, quiet life. Or she has athlete's foot, dandruff, and a smelly body, and she doesn't seem to care. He lies a lot; you had no idea ahead of time! Or she can't make up her mind about anything; she's driving you bonkers.

You said, "For richer, for poorer." In the short time since your wedding, the honeymoon cost you double what you expected; you've both lost your jobs; your father died, and your mother needs financial help; your car died, too, and you're pregnant.

You said, "In sickness and in health." But how could you know she would get new bladder infections every month? How could you know, with that beautiful smile upon his face, that he was one month away from three infected teeth, an ingrown toenail, tonsillitis, and a cyst on his tailbone?

You said. How good is your word? Well, yours is a Christian marriage, patterned after Christ's love for you both, and *He said,* "Surely I will be with you always, to the very end of the age" (Matthew 28:20).

That's His word. And it's good *because of His level of commitment.*

Think about the benefits of that. In all the pressures, you can turn to the Lord. He's your Comfort, your Guide, your Savior, your Protector, your Provider. If He ever cut out on you . . . !

But He won't. *You have His word.*

If things have been bad for you two, the benefits of commitment are actually better than ever. "Hanging in there" will help your partner know your love is real, *your* word is good; you care; you're growing in stability; you can be counted on. It will speak volumes!—that the difficulties are temporary, that better days are ahead *because of your level of commitment.*

Whatever the unpleasant surprises have been, are, or will be, losing your commitment will not be one of them; your mate can count on you through the hard times.

Oh, what comfort! That commitment becomes a wonderful building block for the two of you. No matter what stormy winds may blow, you have the exhilarating feeling that you're going to make it.

Project. Each of you write declarations of your commitment on sheets of paper, and sign them and date them. Read them out loud to each other and then put them in a safe place. Then every time things get rough, you'll have them to get out and read to each other again.

Jesus said, "I will be with you always." You could pattern your promise of commitment on that. Something like:

- "I will be with you, no matter what happens to either of us, as long as we both shall live.

- "If you lose your job, I'll be there.

- "If you become disabled in any way, I'll be at your side.

- "When we're angry at each other, I promise to believe it will work out, and stand with you anyway.

- "When we get bored with each other, I'll ask the Lord for ways to put excitement back into our relationship; I commit myself to keep working at making it better.

- "When things are great I'll be there, too, that all our victories may be shared victories. . . ."

You'll think of lots better ways to say it.
How about putting it into poetry?
Framing them side by side for your bedroom wall?
Sending me copies, so I can rejoice with you too?

11

About Love

You take care of something you love. That only makes sense. If you take good care of your car, it's going to run better. Take good care of your business, and it will return a better profit. Take good care of your body, and you'll stay in better health. Take good care of your wife, and she'll be a better helpmate.[14]

> *I love you,*
> *Not only for what you are,*
> *But for what I am*
> *When I am with you.*
>
> *I love you,*
> *Not only for what*
> *You have made of yourself,*
> *But for what*
> *You are making of me.*
> ROY CROFT[15]

Love is patient, love is kind. It does not envy, it does not boast, it is not proud. It is not rude, it is not self-seeking, it is not easily angered, it keeps no record of wrongs. Love does not delight in evil but rejoices with the truth. It always protects, always trusts, always hopes, always perseveres.

1 Corinthians 13:4–7

A man in love is incomplete until he has married. Then he's finished.

Zsa-Zsa Gabor

If your husband's a nasturtium, you can't make him into a rose. Don't marry him unless you like nasturtiums, and if you're already married, decide nasturtiums are your favorite thing. Then affirm him, encourage him—water and feed and care for him—until he's the most glorious nasturtium in the world.

Someone asked me
To name the time
Our friendship stopped
And love began.

Oh, my darling,
That's the secret,
Our friendship
Never stopped.[16]

Lois Wyse

Anecdote from me:

The couple in our honeymoon hotel room immediately before Ray and me were honeymooners, too: Leopold Stokowski and Gloria Vanderbilt. They were famous and rich; we were unknown and poor. But in that hotel room they must have been as much in love as we were. What happened? Gloria, if you read this, write and tell me.

> *My Jesus, I love Thee.*
> *Thou art to me*
> *Dearer than ever*
> *Charlie can be.*

(Poem composed by C.T. Studd, athlete, missionary, when he married, which he asked his wife to repeat every day!)

> *I love thee with the breath,*
> *Smiles, tears of all my life. And if God choose,*
> *I shall but love thee better after death.*
>
> ELIZABETH BARRETT BROWNING

It's better to have loved and lost than to do forty pounds of laundry a week.

Who I am, what I become, depends largely on those who love me.

JOHN POWELL

The Sevenfold Love of God:

> God loves us with godly love (John 15:9).
> God loves us generously (1 John 3:1).
> God loves us actively, aggressively (Ephesians 2:4,5).
> God loves us whether we deserve it or not (Romans 5:8).
> God loves us sacrificially (Ephesians 5:1,2).
> God loves us joyously (Zephaniah 3:17).
> God loves us without ever changing his mind (Romans 8:38, 39).

A Sevenfold Promise of Love, to be said to each other:

> God helping me, [name], I will love you with godly love.
> I will love you generously.
> I will love you actively, aggressively.
> My love for you will not be based on your merit.
> I will love you sacrificially.
> I will love you joyously.
> And I will never change my mind.

12

Your First Together-Project

Without forgiveness, cleansing and fresh starts, life becomes an endless cycle of resentment and retaliation.

You say daily baths are a "must," don't you, to be presentable to each other.

Daily "quiet times" with God are far more a "must."

If you had to choose, would you rather be freshly showered and in a screaming rage, or be filled with love and peace, not having bathed since yesterday?

Daily Bible study, meditation, and prayer are God's "baths" for your hearts. They'll keep you right with Him and with each other. So it's the first project for your marriage, to be taken with all seriousness. God is the only One to love more than you love each other. Then He's the

only reason to draw apart, to acknowledge His suprem-
acy as you give Him your undivided attention for a piece
of each day.

(I'm thinking right now of our friends brunette John
and red-haired, tennis pro Tina, formerly in a discipling
group with me. They're first-year marrieds, and recently
they sat on our couch telling us how powerful it's been in
their marriage to get up early and meet the Lord before
they meet each other. As they told us, they reached for
each other's hands, and they glowed.)

Husband, it's the way you begin loving your wife as
Christ loves the Church, by washing her in the Word of
God. Make sure your times are faithful and consistent.

For this project together, *first, you have decisions to
make.*

1. *When* will you have your daily quiet times? Mornings? Evenings? (Hopefully at the same time, for account-
ability.)

2. *How?* Certainly separately, the greatest need of all.
But the last part of the period together? Or a different
daily time together?

3. *Where?* Pick separate rooms, with doors if possible.
Then you can each stand, sit, kneel, or get flat on your
faces before God in unself-conscious privacy. Lay the
ground rules; should this be the one time your spouse
should knock before entering?

4. *What tools* will you need?

    A. A complete Bible for each

       In large print

With enough margin space for writing
In a translation you understand (if you buy, con-sider a *New International Version*).

B. A personal notebook[17] for each
About the size of your Bible
If you're picky, in a coordinated color; they'll be used together daily till they wear out!
With sectional dividers

5. *What method will you use?* Divide your quiet time into three parts.

A. *Meditation*
Get quiet before the Lord. Ask Him to shut out all competing thoughts. Perhaps sing a hymn to Him.

B. *Prayer*
Write your daily prayers in the PRAYERS section of your notebook. (See pages 118–121 of my book *Disciplines of the Beautiful Woman,* Word Books, but understand this is a man's method for prayer just as much as a woman's.)
Your prayers will be private, but not incriminat-ing. Write them for the same two reasons I do: you'll know by the dates if you're being truly "daily" about it, and you'll discover the power of God specifically moving in response to what you've prayed about!

Said David:

Morning by morning, O Lord, you hear my voice;

morning by morning I lay my requests before you and wait in expectation.

Psalms 5:3

How exciting and lifting to be in constant touch with the Lord of the universe in this way!

Suggested formula for your daily prayers: ACTS[18]

A doration,

C onfession,

T hanksgiving, and

S upplication (asking Him for things).

Spend about equal time for each part.

All this will be so rich! You will draw so close to God! I can't describe to you in advance how wonderful it will be, for each of you and for your marriage.

> *We kneel, how weak, . . .*
> *We rise, how full of power!*

C. *Bible Study*

Where do you begin? Ray and I, like thousands of others, read through the Bible every year. You can do it if you just read five pages a day—or for helps, subscribe as we do to something like *Seek* magazine[19] or *The Daily Walk.*[20]

Otherwise, start anywhere you want to, but read consecutively, so you get the sense of what you're reading.

If the Bible is new to you, start with Mark or John or maybe Philippians. Wherever you read, don't stop till you're blessed. Whether it's two verses or ten pages, keep going till it gets to you!

Then *ask two questions,* the same two Paul asked on the Damascus road (Acts 22:8,10):

1. *Who are You, Lord?* Write in the BIBLE STUDY section of your notebook all that you learn about Him in this passage.

2. *What shall I do, Lord?* Write down how you need to obey practically what you've read.

Simple habits like these, repeated daily, are life changing: but I warn you, you'll get like Ray. He says he's hooked on his quiet times, and if he doesn't get his daily "fix" he experiences real pain.

When your separate times with the Lord are over, then what? Could you share what you experienced and learned over breakfast? Or in bed at night? "Report times" will get you talking together about the Lord as naturally as you talk about each other. He'll be the best Friend you share in common.

Besides, you need to pray together out loud. If it's a new idea at first, write out your prayers and bow your heads and read them, until you're used to the sound of your own voices. Soon you'll be praying conversationally to Him, back and forth together, and these will be wonderful times for you both.

You're a trio, you know, and if you honor Him in your relationship, He will honor you.

You said that your marriage is founded on Christ the Rock. A religion of mere words is no religion at all. Prove it by constructing on that Rock the crucial cornerstone block of your whole house: your daily quiet times.

13
Temple Gairdner's Prayer Before He Married

That I may come near to her, draw me nearer to Thee than to her;

That I may know her, make me to know Thee more than her;

That I may love her with the perfect love of a perfectly whole heart, cause me to love Thee more than her and most of all.

That nothing may be between me and her, be Thou between us, every moment.

That we may be constantly together, draw us into separate loneliness with Thyself.

And when we meet breast to breast, O God, let it be upon Thine own.[21]

14

For Adults Only: Sex

We should not be ashamed to consider what God was not ashamed to create.

It's true: sex is only for grown-ups.

Immature people can organize housekeeping, hold down jobs, budget and save—do lots of mechanical things really well. But make love?—*really* make love . . .

. . . When it's a driving, tropical hurricane . . .

. . . Or when it's a playtime with tickles and giggles . . .

. . . Or when it's the admiring past words of two best friends . . .

. . . Two bodies, two personalities, two minds in a secret initiation into the mysteries of the deepest human connection ever devised by God; exploring each other and thus exploring Him; serving each other and so serving Him; flowing together in a spiritual wisdom which can discern and separate clothed indecency from naked purity, and fleshly prudery from spiritual revelry ...?

Listen, that's for adults only.

That takes growing past your hang-ups.

Being finished with shyness.

Maturing in your understanding of God.

And having rock-solid confidence in how much you really *like* each other.

Never mind if you're young; it's okay. You can't help when you were born. And if your sex life isn't terrific from the very first, don't be discouraged. Sexual disappointment at the beginning of marriage is so common it's almost normal. Oscar Wilde once said, "Niagara Falls is only the second biggest disappointment of the standard honeymoon." It doesn't mean you're "sexually incompatible."

Look, realize why it's not marvelous right away: anything that great just isn't for amateurs! You never expected to sit down to a piano and play like Paderewski the first time, did you?

Besides, several problems are common ones.

1. *Lack of knowledge.* Read a standard book together, like Dr. Ed and Gaye Wheat's excellent one, *Intended for Pleasure,* published by the Fleming H. Revell Company.

2. *Too much knowledge.* Dr. Alex Comfort wrote, "A little theory makes sex more interesting, more comprehensible, and less scary. *Too much* is a put-down, especially as you're likely to get it out of perspective and become a spectator of your own performance."[22]

Most marrieds these days have been exposed to too much too soon. R-rated movies show all the "techniques" and leave you nothing to discover on your own. Lucky Adam and Eve—they got to wander into the land of love with no map in their hands.

And the way Hollywood shows it, as soon as the two bodies are put together, pow! Friends, in real life it just ain't so. Expect to do a lot of exploring, talking, understanding each other, misunderstanding each other, apologizing—a lot of *living together in an atmosphere of growing mutual respect.*

3. *Leftover feelings from childhood.* But learning to "husband" and to affirm, to "think two"—those other building blocks should gradually shore up this one. Sex is mostly from the neck up.

4. *Fears:* the fear that your sexual organs won't match in size (medical science says this is never—repeat, never—a permanent problem), the fear of unwanted pregnancies, fears of impotence or frigidity—a competent, compassionate doctor or counselor can work through these with you.

5. *Overwork and overbusyness.* When you're pushed, when you're bugged at each other, when you're too tense or too separate—these situations are guaranteed to damage your sex life.

Conclusion: sex will either be miserable or wonderful for you (or on its way to being wonderful) for this reason: in the long run *it will reflect all that you are together.*

(Are you reading this carefully? Of course you are.

There are only two kinds of people in the world, those who are interested in sex and liars.)

Did you know only one one-thousandth or less of sexual relationships in marriage result in making a baby?[23] Then we're not talking reproduction here; we're talking about your physical love together.

Now, get the picture in perspective: if your sex life does not become what it ought to be, your marriage can still survive; sex isn't everything. But it will always be vulnerable; it will have a soft side where Satan can attack. But you don't want merely to survive, do you! You want a great marriage, and for that you must have the strong building block of a happy sex life together.

Sexual skills are interpersonal skills. The more you like each other, the more you understand each other, the closer you are, the better friends you become—the more your sex life will get really good.

And do you know what? Working to make your sex life better will help you to like and understand each other more, get closer, and be better friends!

Then talk it up. "Boy, we make sweet music together." "Wow, you're some lover." You'll be doing yourself a favor, because your partner will begin to feel accepted and to relax and respond—and the things you say will become more and more true.

And love each other constantly with little kindnesses and touches and looks.

I promised myself I wouldn't give you too much advice, so here are just three suggestions:

1. *Don't underrate at first the matter of modesty.* You're legally free to turn the lights up and do what you jolly well please, but what do you *want* to do? Sex together is doing what each other *wants.* ("What can I do to make you happy?")

2. *Expect a difference between male and female timing.* Feminine clocks aren't the same as masculine ones. There was a popular song about wanting a man with a slow hand, an easy touch. That's it.

3. *Don't talk about what you do to anyone else—*not your mother or your best friend. You'll prove you're growing up by this careful code of behavior:

A. When you close your doors, be open about sex.
B. When you open your doors, be closed about sex.

The outside world doesn't need your reports, your advice, your jokes, your chatter. Unless sometime you need the professional advice of a counselor, shield your sex life from all. It's part of what binds you together and helps you "feel married" and "think two." It's your own together-secret.

So enjoy! If it's a burden, it isn't the real thing. God wants to give you a present—a vacation, a holiday every day or night if you want it, a release from all the burdens of living.

Then hurray for sex!

> *And here's the happy, bounding flea;*
> *You cannot tell the he from she—*
> *But she can tell, and so can he.*
>
> ROLAND YOUNG

It's for motivation:

When sex is used and not abused, it exalts the soul and frees the personality for many good works.

It's for giggles:

It's the only game that's never called on account of darkness.

It's for chuckles and belly laughs:

If I told you you have a beautiful body, you wouldn't hold it against me, would you?

DAVID FISHER

And it's for making two people nobler and more fulfilled than they ever could have been if God had not brought them together.

> *You never made*
> *A lamp base out of a Cracker Jack box,*
> *An extra room out of an unused closet,*
> *Or a garden out of a pile of clay.*
> *All you ever made was*
> *A woman out of me.*[24]
>
> LOIS WYSE

15

When You Can't Meet Each Other's Needs, Then What?

"Here are my heart-hungers," you say to each other, whether you say it out loud or not.

"I need love, lots of it, and I need to give it.

"I need to feel that I'm wanted, and that I belong.

"I need to feel that I'm capable of *making it* in my life; I need you to believe in me.

"I need to know that the pleasure my body brings me is permissible and good—that you approve; and that you share in that pleasure, too.

"I need to feel accepted.

"I need to feel understood."

It's really all right to verbalize these things. In fact, it's very important. Start off in these early years building toward a great marriage by *expressing your needs out loud.*

"I need you."

"I need you to need me."

"I need you to say out loud that you love me."

"I need you to touch me and hold me. I need you to kiss me—lots! My mouth gets hungry for that. I need sex with you."

Oh, how miserable life can get when we're shy, or expect our mates to read our minds and know what we want—and then they don't! Then the wall between us builds up higher and higher.

Give your partner the stability, the security of heart that comes when he/she really knows that he's loved, wanted, needed, approved of. Say it and say it in a thousand ways, with both words and deeds. *These are heart needs you're caring for, and each partner must be the guardian of the heart of the other.*

But guess what? You'll never totally meet your partner's needs—and your partner will never totally meet yours. If those are your expectations, you're both in for crashing disappointments.

I can't believe the marriage books I've read that say, "You have the potential for meeting the needs of your mate." Crazy! Impossible! Not even desirable! That leads straight to unrealistic expectations and accusations and frustrations.

Elizabeth Achtemeier says this:

The fallacy of basing the performance of a union on mutual fulfillment of needs alone . . . is illustrated very simply in the following conversation:

HE: Honey, don't be upset. You know I've never found anyone who better meets my needs than you do.

SHE (tearfully): But what if you did?

On that latter question alone many marriages have foundered. Men have found others who have "understood" them better than have their wives. . . . Women have been introduced to males who have made them feel more "important". . . .[25]

Only God deep, deep down understands you: your personality, your background, your feelings, your cravings, your needs. He made you; only He totally knows you. And for your deepest heart cravings, He is the only Source. Both of you must go back, back, back to Him.

Sometimes Ray says to me, "Anne, I thought I understood you, and you've completely got me guessing. I guess I'll never really comprehend that feminine mystique."

He's right. I even kinda like it that way. I think I'll slip behind my silk veil. . . .

And much as he loves me, he can miss my needs a country mile—partly because I'm no doubt poor at communicating them, and partly because I don't always understand what they are myself.

Listen: the more you relate first to God, in "practicing His presence," in daily quiet times, in public worship— the more deeply satisfied you'll be. And having your own needs met by Him, you can quit being self-centered and start being concerned about your partner.

Aha! We just stumbled onto the crux of this need-meeting thing. Trust God to meet yours, and you'll be more able to meet your spouse's. And vice versa.

Hebrews 7:26 explains where human needs are finally met:

Such a high priest [as Christ] meets our need—one who is holy, blameless, pure, set apart from sinners, exalted above the heavens.

Ray and I are satisfied people. Our private fellowship with God sees to that. There are places where we irritate each other or misunderstand each other. Then Ray must flee to God for the comfort and instructions he needs. I must flee to the same God—but separately, telling Him all about it and seeing what to do.

When all is said and done, each person is left alone with his God, the Well from which to draw and draw and draw.

Then from our withdrawals for fresh supply, Ray and I come back and fall into each other's arms.

Special moments come to mind. Like last week when Bill and Gloria Gaither were on stage leading us in singing,

I am loved, I am loved,
I can risk loving you,
For the One who knows me best loves me most.

> *I am loved, I am loved,*
>   *Won't you please take my hand...?*[26]

... and in the dark Ray was softly, gently kissing my fingers and my hand over and over until the sensuousness of it was almost a gorgeous ache looming there before me in the dark.

Take a Break: Et Ceteras About Marriage

PART I: TO-DO CALENDAR FOR YOUR FIRST MARRIED YEAR

A. Immediately following the honeymoon:

1. Sit down and talk together about your two schedules and your new life-style. How can you "eliminate and concentrate"? Deuteronomy 24:5 says, "If a man has recently married, he must not be sent to war or have any other duty laid on him. For one year he is to be free to stay home and bring happiness to the wife he has married"!

2. You have notebooks for your quiet times. Buy calendar pages to go in each of these notebooks.[27] Every Sunday sit down and coordinate your coming week together. Mark in CHURCH, QUIET TIMES,

TIMES TOGETHER, SOCIAL AND OTHER EVENTS (kept to a minimum), JOBS, SHOPPING, LAUNDRY, HOUSECLEANING, and so forth, deciding who does what on a trial basis. Check each other, that neither is too overscheduled. (As new appointments are filled in during the week, every Sunday check these over to make sure the other has them marked in. Even if the other is not involved, he/she needs to know where you are.)

B. *At three months:*

Make sure all thank-you notes for wedding gifts and kindnesses have been finished.

C. *At six months:*

1. Write a letter to the pastor who married you, thank him again, and let him know how you're doing.

2. What about having a godly older couple over for dinner and ask them questions that have come up so far, and get advice?

D. *At eleven months:*

Plan your first anniversary celebration. Be sure you both love what you decide to do. It may or may not cost money: hike in the woods with picnic? Monopoly on the floor in front of the fire? Go to an amusement

park? Overnight somewhere? Could it include a little
ceremony of prayer and recommitment?

E. *At end of year before anniversary:*

What needs to be repaired or caught up on?. Something around the house? A broken friendship? A word
or deed for which you need to apologize? A bill which
needs paying off? A closet or cupboard which needs
cleaning out? A letter written to a friend? Parents over
for a nice dinner? Is there something unsaid between
the two of you which needs to be made right before
the new year begins? (This inventory-taking would be
a neat way to end each married year, to start out the
next one better.)

F. *On First Anniversary:*

Hopefully you've had a full year to think only "two."
Now spend at least an hour discussing how you'd like
to turn outward to help others—separately, together,
or both. Sunday-school class teaching? Regular visits
to an old people's home, a children's hospital? Some
ministry to the poor? A short trip to serve overseas
missions?

Love does not consist in gazing at each other but
in looking outward together in the same direction.
ANTOINE DE SAINT EXUPERY

PART II: GOOD QUOTES, BAD JOKES

God puts us in a binding relationship that we cannot get out of—like a vise. If we stay in that vise He can turn up the fire, burn off the dross, purify the gold, and transform our lives.

DEL FEHNSENFELD, JR.[28]

Marriage is like a mousetrap; those who are out are trying to get in, and those who are in are trying to get out.

A large woman struggling to climb into a bus glared at her husband and said, "John, you're not as gallant as you were when you were a boy." "No," he said, "and you're not as buoyant as you were when you were a gal!"

When singleness is bliss, 'tis folly to be wives.

BILL COUNSELMAN

You didn't walk into a "marriage trap"; your free will made the choice. The wedding vow was full of your "will":

"*X, Will* you have *Y* to be your lawfully wedded wife, and *will* you honor her and keep her, and so forth?"

And you answered, "I *will.*"

"And, *Y, Will* you have *X . . .* ?"

Getting married is a voluntary thing.

JUDGE: I understand you and your wife had some words.

HUSBAND: Well, I had some, but I never got a chance to get them in.

> There's only one thing for a man to do who's married to a woman who enjoys spending money, and that's to enjoy earning it.
>
> ED HOWE

The husband watched football on TV on Friday night. He watched two football games on Saturday. He watched two more games on Sunday.

His wife said, "You love football more than you love me."

"Yes," he said, "but you come ahead of basketball."

The Old Testament shows the variety of marriage:

Adam and Eve: she got them into sin, and their children turned out mixed good and bad;

Colorless Isaac with bossy, conniving Rebekah;

But Abraham with his gorgeous Sarah—now, there was a match. A man of faith with a faithful wife (1 Peter 3:6), separated only by death, and that after many years (Genesis 23:1).

PART III: ABOUT RAY AND ME

He was twenty-one, a Navy man on campus, and the quarterback and captain of our football team. The campus paper called him, "Rugged Ray Ortlund, the blond bombshell of the University of Redlands." He pulled from the breast pocket of his uniform his little Testament and Psalms, and asked me to marry him as he shared Psalm 34:3, "O magnify the Lord with me, and let us exalt his name together."

There was the sunny afternoon in the park when he wrestled me down on my back on the grass (he thought you're supposed to treat brides the way you treat your brothers), and to get him off me I slapped his face—*hard.*

There was the way he looked in civilian clothes (I'd never seen him out of either his Navy or his football uniforms until our wedding), going off to classes for his senior year of college. He wore new *glasses,* an open-collared shirt, slipover sweater, gray flannel slacks, and saddle shoes. Oh, he looked *so cute,* and I felt so klutzy, and I wondered if he were secretly disappointed that he hadn't married some doll-baby like Abigail Furness.

There was the Sunday morning I tried out our new pressure cooker while we went to church, and came home to discover both cooker and dinner burned black. I opened the back door and threw the whole thing into a snowbank and refused to retrieve it. I'd come from a home where the maid didn't use a pressure cooker, so how could I know about things like that? Ray had come from a home where you never threw anything away. In the spring when our pressure cooker appeared through the melting snows, Ray got it and scrubbed it, and we used it as a regular cooking pan.

There was the day when Ray explained to me that he'd

read my pregnancy nausea was all in my head, that throwing up was an unconscious attempt on the part of the mother-to-be to expel her baby. *Oh,* I wanted to punch him out.

There was my misery when we visited Ray's big family in Iowa, and he reverted to his "Ortlund brother" personality, boisterous and macho. He seemed strange, and suddenly not all mine anymore. I felt left out. And I felt incompetent as a mother: I couldn't get the hang of diaper pinning, and of all the baby cousins, mine was the only one whose diapers kept falling off. And I also felt awkward and stiff and overdressed. The Abigail Furness thing hit me again, and I wondered if Ray was sorry he'd chosen me.

There was the afternoon when Ray stopped the car in the middle of some lively, high-pitched debating on my part, and he asked me why my personality had changed; and if having three babies in our first three and a half years of marriage had contributed to my becoming more keyed-up and aggressive and nervous and dominating. I cried, and I said I thought it had.

There were the years of being overwhelmed by his incredible physical vigor and my total inability to keep up with him (we'd go on vacations, and he'd want to run, and I'd want to sleep); and of wondering if he were secretly disappointed in me because I wasn't constantly at his side, sharing his stamina and sports and fun.

There were the many years, unknown to me, when he wondered if deep down I wasn't disappointed in *him,* in his early lack of finesse. Ray's built-in inferiority complex, which has faded over the years, fed his conviction that he could never match me in "class" (?), and that I secretly thought I could have done better.

And through the years he looked so *cute,* and was so loved by evergrowing numbers, and always he was in forward motion, working for new goals and dreaming new dreams. . . . *Was I just a tagalong,* I wondered?

Ray and Anne, pastoring and raising children, smiling and busy and loving each other, and so proud of each other—and both of us secretly feeling unworthy and not quite accepted. We had a good marriage but with just a tiny sadness at the core of it. We were aware of it in our behind-the-scenes life together, which was kind and polite and a little shy.

Polite! That was Ray. *It was a building block to greatness,* and neither of us knew it. He was full of little tendernesses, opening doors for me, helping me, *noticing me.* It made me want to remember to say, "Thank you," and treat him in kind. And in spite of our mistaken insecurities, the habit of courtesy built us ever more strongly together.

Don't think our marriage was all built on that one block. And we have misunderstood each other and hurt each other a lot; in thirty-eight years you do everything *a lot.*

But a few years ago our schedule changed and some pressures were off, and suddenly we had the time and concentration to discover our true hearts. We opened up to each other in surprise and joy. *He really likes me,* just the way I am. Forget Abigail Furness! *And I'm crazy about him;* I've always been, but now he's really convinced.

Ray, I'll see you later today. . . . I'm writing high over the Pacific Ocean, flying home from speaking in the Philippines, and you have just arrived home from speaking in Washington. Wait for me, I'm coming . . . !

We've come full circle, enough for me to see that our early years, for all their goofs, got us ready for what we're now experiencing.

The right building blocks were going into place.

16

Your Rights, Your Partner's Rights

Probably no one has told you what your partner's rights are, and your partner should never have to ask you for them.

And yet there is no one in the world who can fulfill them except you. So read these rights with care.

To the Wife

1. Your husband has a right to sexual satisfaction.
If you receive him, if you eagerly accept him, both sexually and emotionally, both his body and his person, *the way he is*—you're almost assured of giving him his due right of sexual satisfaction. If there's any problem beyond this, see a doctor. Spare nothing to make sure this right is fully his.

2. He has a right to intellectual companionship. During courtship days anything you talked about was good enough—the "tingle" between you kept it alive.

But from now on you may have to work at it. He has a right to compatibility with you, and probably he will not get too jazzed over your recital of how you mended the sleeve of the ironing board or what you said to the girl in your aerobics class.

I read one time that Washington is full of brilliant men and the women they married when they were young and immature. What a shame! Determine to grow up with your husband.

3. If he earns a salary, then he has a right to economic security. Only when he's jobless is this principle not in force. Otherwise, he will earn what he can—and the bulk of the spending will probably be up to you. Then it's up to you not to overspend, not to live too close to the limit, without a margin for emergencies. He's bringing home what he can; he has a right to peace of mind in what happens to it. So whether there are two salaries or one, it's you who must take the initiative to tithe, to save, and to live *under your means.*

4. He has a right to a home. He may be a "wandering Armenian," but his maleness deeply hankers for a place to come back to where he is king.

Take seriously how he thinks his home should be. If you insist on having the home totally *your* way, he may feel like a stranger coming home to your house, and so eventually go home to someone else's.

The world is a cruel place, fast-paced and competitive. It dumps its casualties without a pang, and even to survive is to suffer. Then let his home be the place he comes back to to be loved, admired, listened to, and followed—the place of his healing and restoration.

5. *He has a right to children.* A man's offspring may seem to him one of his few contributions to his world—perhaps his only contribution. But if they've been well loved and raised and managed (probably mostly by you), he can lift up his head.

If you can't have natural children, consider adopting; the world is full of little ones with no place to go. And because Ray and I have both produced and adopted children, let me assure you there's no difference in your love for them or your sense of pride of accomplishment over getting them raised.

So don't say too long that you're having too much fun, that it's too soon, that you can't afford a baby yet. The time will never really seem the best time. Don't wait too long to deny him something a man fundamentally longs for.

> I remember that Coleridge somewhere speaks about the death of a man who has no children—it seems so final, he remarks, so much like being "wiped out." . . .
>
> Why don't we teach our children to look more frequently at the long, unbroken line of ancestors behind them, and to look forward to the potentiality of an unbroken line of descendants, made possible through their own marriage? To me, it's positively thrilling![29]

To the Husband

1. Like you, she has a right to sexual satisfaction. There was a day when only husbands were supposed to achieve climaxes—but now we know that was silly. She, too, longs for deep sexual fulfillment—but she can fake it better than you if she doesn't get it.

First Peter 3:7 talks about a wife's three rights, and it says, live with your wife "according to knowledge" (KJV). Study her, get to know her thoroughly. Get to know what makes her tick—and "ticked"!

This word "knowledge" or "know" in the Scriptures can have deeper connotations than those we usually think of: "Adam knew Eve his wife; and she . . . bare Cain" (Genesis 4:1 KJV). Live with your wife "according to knowledge." Know the tender words, hugs, romantic touches day and night that she needs (though you may not) as prelude to sex. And in your marriage bed get to know the specific caresses and pressures and timing that she requires to bring her to climax. Ask her and *ask her!* It will take as long as you live, but get to be the world's greatest authority on your wife and what turns her on. It will be your private knowledge, but she has the right to expect you to learn it.

2. She has a right to be "respected as the weaker partner," as First Peter 3:7 says. There's a lot of talk about sexual equality these days, and modern women often seem so strong, you may feel intimidated.

But womankind carries a special pressure you will never carry: she can get pregnant. For all her big talk about careers and independence, *you threaten her.* She needs from you a sense of leadership and protection and control, that you can earn enough money for all of you if she has a baby, that you're strong enough to maintain equilibrium if she weakens, that you will be there to uphold her if ever her knees buckle.

She pays a terrific price, being a modern woman. She's expected to hold a job perfectly, keep a house perfectly, always look perfect, and eventually raise perfect children. The media all say she can do it!—but she knows deep inside she can't.

Well, notice again First Peter 3:7: "Treat [her] with respect as the weaker partner. . . ." Uphold her in her role, reassure her.

3. She has a right to be treated as an heir with you of the gracious gift of life (1 Peter 3:7). You did not inherit a bigger chunk of living than she did. She deserves to taste all that you taste and smell all you smell and feel all you feel. She deserves to have you share with her what you experience when you're apart from her—and to have your full attention when she shares what she experienced apart from you.

It's her right to have all her gifts developed, not to be thwarted in any way just because she's married. 'Way back in 1850 a woman named Lucy Stone wrote this:

Do not tell us before we are born, even, that our province is only to cook dinners, darn stockings, and sew on buttons. I know not what you believe of God, but I believe He gives yearnings and longings to be filled, and that He did not mean all our time should be devoted to feeding and clothing the body.

But only you can encourage her fulfillment. She is indeed under your authority. If you hold her down she'll be frustrated—but she'll also feel guilty if she tries to break loose. From the start, husband, treat her as a co-heir with you in all the business of living fully. Don't deny her her right.

And this amazing verse First Peter 3:7, ends with what happens if you give your wife these three rights: then *your own prayers won't be hindered.*

Apparently, if you grant your wife's desires, God will grant yours. And if you don't, He may not!

17

What Goals Do for You

Idealists . . . foolish enough to throw caution to the winds . . . have advanced mankind and have enriched the world.
EMMA GOLDMAN

Redbook magazine recently asked 730 marriage counselors for the ten most common problems that pull couples apart. Here they are, listed in order of their frequency:

1. Breakdown in communication
2. Loss of shared goals or interests
3. Sexual incompatibility
4. Infidelity
5. Excitement and fun gone out of marriage
6. Money problems
7. Conflicts about children

125

8. Alcohol and drug abuse
9. Woman's equality issues
10. In-laws

When Wayne Rickerson, family pastor of the First Christian Church of Napa, California, read these, he was surprised that numbers 2 and 5 were so high on the list. Why should there be so much "loss of shared goals or interests" and so little excitement and fun left in marriage? In his book *We Never Have Time for Just Us*,[30] Pastor Rickerson writes that after thinking about it for a while, he realized he shouldn't have been surprised.

Reason: we're in the "independence" era, and there can't be shared projects if the married partners are each just occupied with self-fulfillment. "This kind of thinking will, of course, lead to the decline of fun, excitement, and shared goals and interests in marriage."

Then why shouldn't the reverse be true, that going after goals together will become another building block toward a great marriage?

When Ray and I were early marrieds he began saying, "Anne, let's make some new points of departure." Somehow that was his expression for short-term goals. Every so often, when he was feeling itchy to stretch more, we'd make some new "points of departure": lose five pounds, think about attributes of God for three minutes daily, cull the ratty clothes out of our closets, or whatever. He'd print them on cards to put over our mirror and on the car visor. When we went to England to pastor a church for a summer, we put our points of departure into verse:

"Stand up straight, watch your weight, keenly appreciate!" We still say that one to each other.

God loves your desire to improve!—especially to improve together. *He helps you do what honors Him the most,* as Psalm 23:3 says in *The Living Bible.*

For the past few years I've fast-walked up and down hills for thirty minutes five mornings a week. But last year I was working hard on a book deadline, and for several weeks I didn't walk at all. When I started again, I was amazed how I puffed on the hills, and how sore my legs were the next day.

I didn't have to do anything to get out of shape; it just happened naturally when I quit exercising.

The same thing happens in any marriage! *If you just go along without effort* and let time pass, your relationship will go downhill. Your love will sag, your communication will go—and so will the excitement and fun in your marriage. It takes constant work, time, commitment, and strategizing to keep your marriage in shape!

Now it's time to "do the truth":

1. Sit down together and set some goals.

2. Make them together-goals that involve you both.

3. Make them visible and measurable, so you can tell if you achieved them or not.

4. Determine by what date you'll have them accomplished.

5. Don't make too many at once; three or four should be maximum.

6. Don't make them so difficult that you get discouraged; bite off smaller chunks at first to get started.

> *It's hard*
> *By the yard,*
> *But a cinch*
> *By the inch.*

7. Hold each other accountable to achieve your goals. Pray over them, talk about them.

8. When they're achieved, set new ones!

This is the time to begin. Make some lists of possible goals separately at first, and put stars by the ones you want the most. Now compare what you put down. With a true desire to reach the *other's* goals before your own, decide together on two, three, or four for starters.

When the set date arrives, did you make your goals? Do you need to extend the time for any, or set them aside and come back to them later?

Suggested possibilities for goals:

1. Read your Bibles and pray together [how many] times a week.

2. Say "I love you" every day for [how many] days in a row.

3. The house straightened up by the time you both leave in the morning for [how many] days in a row.

4. Take a certain class together.

5. Start a savings account by [date]. Have in it [so many dollars] by [further date].

6. Take up a certain sport together; play it [how often].

7. Laundry done and house cleaned by Saturday night, so you can truly relax Sundays and/or have company over [how many] consecutive weeks.

"A journey of a thousand miles," says an old Chinese proverb, "begins with just one step."

Shared goals will help keep you "thinking two."

And shared goals will keep your fun and excitement going.

18

Money: Make All You Can, Save All You Can, Give All You Can

Money is a terrible master but an excellent servant.

P.T. BARNUM, 1810–1891
Founder of Barnum and Bailey Circus

A young husband went to a psychiatrist and said, "I have two gorgeous condominiums, each with pool, spa, and tennis court—one in Orange County and one in Palm Springs. My wife and I each have Jaguars, which is our favorite car, and we belong to a neat golf club, and we eat out so well our Diner's Club bill averages fifteen hundred dollars a month."

"So what's your problem?" asked the psychiatrist.

The fellow said, "I only make a hundred dollars a week."

That's a problem! And that's "the big one" with lots and lots of early marriages. They're spending *over* their budget instead of *under* it, and you can just count on the result: tensions, worry, accusations, arguments.

Robert Blood says, "Despite the highest incomes in the world, Americans quarrel over money more than anything else"[31]—and even if you're not American you could have caught the disease.

Here's another result of Blood's studies: "Whereas in-law problems are concentrated at the beginning of marriage and child-rearing problems in the middle, financial conflicts spread over the whole life cycle, taking new forms as circumstances change."[32]

Usually what wrecks married couples isn't the "high cost of living" but "the cost of living high." It's wanting too much too soon, getting used to little or big luxuries that ought to wait till later. And all those businesses out there are urging you to have it before you can pay for it.

John Wesley said it first: *Make all you can, save all you can, and give all you can.* Fix your spending into this overall three-way plan, and you'll have forged an important building block toward a great marriage.

Make all you can. Money isn't "the root of all evil"— only the *love* of money is (1 Timothy 6:10). Money can be used for great blessing and for God's glory—in the hands of the right people.

So how do you "make all you can"? God spells out

how in the Book of Proverbs (and for money manage-
ment you ought to read the whole book of Proverbs in
The Living Bible). He says it's by hard work:

> Lazy men are soon poor; hard workers get rich.
> 10:4
> Lazy people want much but get little, while the
> diligent are prospering. 13:4
> Work brings profit; talk brings poverty! 14:23
> If you love sleep, you will end in poverty. Stay
> awake, work hard, and there will be plenty to eat!
> 20:13

And what will you do with your money?

Save all you can. I just saw a great quotation: "Plan
ahead. It wasn't raining when Noah built the ark."

From the first of your marriage (don't wait until you can
afford it), *give to the Lord the 10 percent or more you've
agreed on together.* You may groan, "We'll never see that
money again!" Listen, that's the only money you ever *will*
see again! Jesus says:

> "Do not store up for yourselves treasures on earth,
> where moth and rust destroy, and where thieves
> break in and steal. But store up for yourselves trea-
> sures in heaven, where moth and rust do not destroy,
> and where thieves do not break in and steal."
>
> MATTHEW 6:19, 20

For yourselves, He says. Every penny you give Him He
converts into your eternal bank account, multiplying and

waiting for you in heaven. It's a more wonderful and important system than we can possibly imagine in this life.

Don't wait to start later. At least tithe (that's giving Him 10 percent of your income) from your wedding day on.

And then give yourselves another 10 percent. Out of even modest paychecks, put away a regular amount into a savings account, something very safe. (This isn't the time to speculate.)

No matter what the inflation rate tries to tell you, Proverbs 22:7 says, "Just as the rich rule the poor, so the borrower is servant to the lender" (TLB). This monthly payment to yourselves will help you buy most of your needs with cash. It will save you unbelievable amounts of tension as well as interest payments. (Ralph Waldo Emerson said it: "Money often costs too much.") Besides, it will give you financial room to breathe, money to give as needs arise, and opportunities to do all sorts of wonderful, creative things.

We're talking budget now, and that's not easy when you're starting out; you're shooting in the dark. But really, two groups of people must keep a budget: newlyweds who haven't had a chance yet to test their ability to live within their incomes, and anybody temporarily in trouble, or just wanting to save more.

(Ray and I haven't lived by a written-out budget for years, but these very six months we are, when we're going through a tight time. It's important for us right now to monitor exactly our income and outgo, and have a strong sense of control.)

Plan your budget together. Everything must be in one

pot, both your debts and your assets. *Marriage is oneness in everything.* If you both work, income is "ours." Hardly notice who earns the most. And budget decisions are "ours": everything that goes into the pot comes out of it by mutual agreement, "submitting to one another" (*see* Ephesians 5:21).

Budget manuals explain, if you need them, about marking out fixed items first. These would include:

A. To the Lord
B. To yourselves (savings)
C. Rent or mortgage payments
D. Utilities, etc.

And then working with what's left over, according to what you both feel is important.

You've just made your goals together; do any of them involve money? Adjust your budget accordingly.

When Ray and I began—boy, was our style primitive! We cashed our paycheck on payday. We divided up the cash into envelopes marked CHURCH, FOOD, CAR, CLOTH-ING, etc. placed in a dresser drawer. When one envelope was empty, that was it until another payday put money in it again. We had no credit cards, no debts; we were incredibly happy, and more incredibly, we were never robbed!

But something began to happen along the way. *We learned we didn't have to spend everything marked for spending.* The first four years for us were tough with Ray in school, me not working, and one, two, then three babies arriving; but when, after four years, he graduated from Princeton Seminary to pastor his first church, we had eight hundred incredible dollars stashed away toward furniture and our first washing machine.

Today our system of finances is a little more sophisticated, but the principle has been ingrained into us, to *spend under our budget*. Even in our midthirties with three junior-high children, when we came to a large church, bought a big home and were in the public eye, our sixteen-by-thirty-foot living room had minimal furniture in it for two years, until we could pay cash for more.

Oh, the peace this has kept in our hearts! It's been a great building block for our solid, loving relationship!

You say you just can't spend under your budget? Here's a checklist for suggestions:

A. Buy where you get the quality you want at the lowest prices.

B. I said "the quality you want" because many purchases don't have to be good quality. Try to buy a good bed; quality tables and lamps can come later.

C. List what you hope to buy in the next six months. Then start saving, comparing, and asking about coming sales.

D. Pay cash for everything possible.

E. Buy secondhand. (You get houses and probably cars that way, why not furniture and clothes? I know a gorgeous mother with four children in private schools. Few people know she gets everything except shoes and undies at "next-to-new" shops, and she looks terrific.)

F. Keep a wise balance between buying goods and experiences. You need some of both. But early-married couples who go to too many restaurants and movies may struggle to buy appliances or a car.

G. Do you have to have a daily paper? Can you turn your hot-water heater lower? What can you buy in bulk? And so on and so on. . . .

Well, until living by a budget becomes automatic, communicate. Keep your heads together; even write your checks together; or at least stay agreed and stay knowledgeable about what's in the pot, what's coming out of it, and what's left.

And if you need financial advice, get it! Don't muddle along and get into worse trouble. See a financial counselor—or a godly older couple who know how to live right.

Give all you can. Let me tell you about our friends Dave and Lori. Dave put himself through four years of college and four more of seminary, and started into his first job as an assistant pastor in a church. Then he married Lori. Total assets: his old Ford, her older Volkswagen bug, and a very few hundred dollars in the bank. They paid for their own wedding.

From the first they had an unusual system. They needed a washing machine, so they saved until they had the total price, gave the money to the Lord, and looked to see how He would provide a washing machine! No one knew their need except God, and of course He provided.

Then they wanted a sewing machine: they saved up the price, gave the money to Him, and prayed. Out of the blue came a sewing machine. And so on!

It's ten years later; Dave and Lori are in their midthirties. Dave is pastoring his own small church; they have only his modest salary and now two daughters. They're even still driving the same Ford and beat-up VW bug! But they're buying not only their own home but a rental property besides, and they have investments all over. They've never had a debt except their mortgage debts; they've given heavily to the Lord, and they're happy as clams. Dave's and Lori's handling of money has been a strong building block in what's becoming a truly great marriage.

That system probably won't be your system (it isn't ours), but you need to see several reasons why money is such a special consideration:

1. *God creates and owns all money and all material things.* He says, "I have no need of your gifts to Me. I own everything." "If I were hungry I would not tell you, for the world is mine, and all that is in it" (*see* Psalms 50:9–12).

2. *God distributes money and material things as He*

chooses. Humans and all living things are absolutely de-
pendent on His distribution. "These all look to [God] to
give them their food at the proper time" (Psalms 104:27).

3. *God knows that in the human heart, money is His great
rival*—that it's either/or. "You cannot serve both God
and Money" (Matthew 6:24). "Some people, eager for
money, have wandered from the faith . . ." (1 Timothy
6:10).

4. *One of God's clearest promises is to keep His children
supplied.* "My God will meet all your needs according to
his glorious riches in Christ Jesus" (Philippians 4:19).
(And *see* Psalms 37:25.)

5. *God tests your faith by asking you to give to Him first,
before you are sure of His supply.* "Seek first his kingdom
and his righteousness, and all these [material] things will
be given to you as well" (Matthew 6:33). "Give, and it
will be given to you . . ." (Luke 6:38).

Money is a powerful way God seeks to build two things
into your life:

1. *Compassion.* He wants you to be sensitive to the suf-
fering "have-nots." "A generous man will himself be
blessed, for he shares his food with the poor" (Proverbs
22:9).

2. *Faith.* You'll grow in your confidence in Him and
peace of mind on every issue, when you honor Him by
tithing or more. You'll also feel close to Him, and you'll
have a sense of obedience—that you're doing your part,
so you expect Him to do His!

We know a couple who were tearing around on a Sunday morning getting breakfast dishes done and two babies ready so they could leave for Sunday school, and the kitchen sink stopped up. This was panic time, because company was coming for dinner, right after church.

Dennis looked at that yukky sink, and he looked up to heaven, and he complained, "God, I tithed!"

Immediately the sink went "SH-SH-SHLUP" and it was clear. (So help me, that's a true story.)

One last word about money: *don't mind if you don't have much.* It makes you creative.

Like the December in our early marriage when funds were low, and I sneaked Ray's pullover sweater out of his drawer, and for three dollars had it dyed bottle green, and wrapped it and gave it back to him for Christmas.

I can't tell you how tickled I was to see the look of genuine delight on his face.

Project: Have you made out a budget? Do it now. You already have? Then do a study on money in the Bible. Write your own principles on money from each of the following passages:

1. Psalms 50:9–12

2. Psalms 104:21–29

3. Matthew 7:24; 1 Timothy 6:10

4. Philippians 4:19; Psalms 37:25

5. Matthew 6:33; Luke 6:38

19

Outside Relationships: Delightful or Dangerous?

Behind every achievement are two: a proud spouse and a surprised mother-in-law.

"Ortie," I said to my guru, "let me pick your brains for my book. What shall I write about in-laws?"

He lowered his eyelids and puffed on his water pipe, while a sense of the wisdom of the ages pervaded the room.

No, he didn't; he wouldn't know a water pipe from a plumber's friend. Actually he scooped me up in his arms and tickled me with his chin and said, "Don't have any."

"What? Don't have any in-laws? Only Adam and Eve didn't have any in-laws."

"Well, then, have 'em three thousand miles away, the

way we did." (That's more or less true. We started our married life in Tacoma, Washington, with our parents in the Midwest and on the East Coast. It worked out great, and it certainly fit in with Genesis 2:24 about leaving father and mother.)

"Come on," I said. "Get serious."

He put me down and thought.

"It's important to appreciate each other's background, to try to understand it and not demean it or negate it. A bride's parents and customs and background in general are mostly what she brings to her marriage—a first marriage, at least. They make up who she is at that point. Criticizing any of that will just make her defensive and hostile, or at least uncomfortable. She probably wants to remain loyal. The word in Scripture to honor your parents also means honoring the parents of your mate."

Isn't it interesting that in Genesis 2:24 when God said, supposedly to Adam and Eve, "For this reason a man will leave his father and mother and be united to his wife . . ." this was spoken to all *but* Adam and Eve! They didn't have any parents; He was saying it for the benefit of all those to follow.

And a great benefit it is, too, to *get away*. Better a shabby apartment with freedom to adjust to each other, than to live in luxury too close to parents who try to manage you.

Parents are over-anxious, sometimes over-curious, usually over-eager for you to get everything right the first time. But you need to make your own decisions, good or bad. For twenty-plus or -minus years you were to make them happy; now you're to make your partner happy. *Don't confuse the old life with the new life.*

"What can I do to make you happy?" is the key question to ask of your partner. But if you're simultaneously asking the same question of your parents or anyone else, there's going to be conflict and anxiety.

Ephesians 6:1,2 spells out the difference in relationship between "little child"-parent and "grown-child"-parent.

> Verse 1: Children [little ones], obey your parents in the Lord, for this is right.

Then comes a command for offspring of all ages:

> Verse 2: Honor your father and mother—which is the first commandment with a promise. . . .

That is, it's the first one of the Ten Commandments, given through Moses in Exodus 20, which has a promise attached:

> . . . That it may go well with you and that you may enjoy long life on the earth.

You're to respect them, appreciate them, be thoughtful of them, care for them if need arises (1 Timothy 5:8), but not any longer to obey them. That was only when you were a child under their authority, and it ceased on your wedding day.

"Honoring" certainly includes considering their opinions; they may be a lot wiser than you. But having considered them, then make your own final decisions, before the Lord and with each other.

We had dinner recently with a pastor and his wife. Joe said, "I married a couple four months ago that I thought were sure winners. They seemed obviously in love; they talked about the Lord openly and their desire to have a Christ-centered marriage; they're faithful churchgoers and they're from good homes. Can you believe this? Four months, and they're getting a divorce! Apparently young Rex is unhealthily attached to his father. They work together in business, and she says he's so totally involved with his father that he can't give time or allegiance to her. She's an emotional wreck. I'm just shocked! I thought they'd have a great marriage."

If fathers-in-law are threatening for a new marriage, mothers-in-law are worse. I am one, so hear it from me. There's a reason for our bad reputation: mothers, more than fathers, tend to be overpossessive and meddling, just as young wives, more than young husbands, tend to be overdependent and clinging.

Studies show that marriages are generally healthier when parents get together with their newly married children only once a week or several times a month. There's a sharp drop in the number of happily married couples when the contact with parents is oftener than once a week.

On a scale of *one* to *ten* (*one* being "ignoring" and *ten* being "overpossessive"), how would you rate your parents? Your parents-in-law? Think about it. How would you rate your own behavior with each set—*one* being "cold shoulder" and *ten* being "insecure clinging"?

If your marriage is new or fairly new, you're probably in the transitional problems of learning to "leave and cleave."[33] But your ratings of their behavior and your own will help determine just how you "honor" them—whether at a distance with loving notes, cards, and gifts on special days, or whether with happy double dates and freely asking them their opinions.

If your own or your partner's behavior is on the high side in "clinging," there will need to be some talking through between the two of you, and lots of assurances and tender, loving care. And maybe signing an agreement which spells out the new status:

I AM NO LONGER ACCOUNTABLE TO OBEY MY PARENTS. I AM FREED FROM THAT AUTHORITY, TO BE BOUND, JOYFULLY AND SECURELY, TO MY MATE.

Maybe in-laws aren't the problem; friends are. The husband remains so close to his old gang that he wants to keep tearing around with them, being a little boy. Or the wife has a special girl friend who has *always* known *all* her secrets. . . .

Go back and read chapter 6 again and start to "think two." And let me tell you how easily this can become a problem.

I remember many years ago a gal that Ray and I thoroughly enjoyed. And there was no doubt that she and Ray were on a special wavelength in joke telling and giggling over funny things. It didn't bother me, and none of us realized that another woman was eyeing the two of them with great nervousness. In all innocence they were getting their reputations into trouble—and especially Ray, being this woman's pastor.

How did the thing get resolved? Well, in a few months Ray and I had a romantic renaissance. Our marriage was never bad, but all relationships ebb and flow, and we simply came into another great time of hand-holding and hugs and touches, which this woman couldn't help but notice. It totally relieved her worry that her pastor was up to something. Years later she told us about it.

So let me give you this building block, which will add strategically in the construction of that great marriage you're building: *keep everyone assured of how in love you are.* Outside relationships can get close without danger, if your own relationship is obviously much closer yet.

Let your love be visible and audible! Let your attention to each other in public be sustained until it's ingrained habit. Then you can be as warm and friendly to others as you want, and you can thoroughly enjoy your family and friends.

Keep it obvious that you two are in love.
Obvious to each other.
And obvious to the rest of the world.

20

The Technique of Red-Carpet Welcomes

The Church eagerly awaits the return of Christ, right? That's part of love: "When we're apart I miss you! I'm incomplete without you; hurry to me soon!" ". . . Come, Lord Jesus" (Revelation 22:20).

So you need to celebrate, at least sometimes, your reunions after separations. Show that you missed your partner. Do something that says, "I've been anticipating your return. I missed you, and I'm so glad you're home!"

Especially in our early years we really worked at this. Ray was usually the one out for evening meetings, so I'd get ready for him. At various times—

1. I turned the lights down, put on soft music, and glided into his arms when he got inside the door;

2. I laid his pajamas over an easy chair, and had a program he liked going on television;

3. I waited until he got all the way into bed, and had a game of Chinese checkers hidden under the sheets. ...

Don't do it every time, or the surprise element is gone and you've put yourself under the law.

But sometimes when he comes home from work for dinner, when she comes home after an evening out— what can you spring on your mate that says, "I've been preparing for your coming; I'm so glad you're here"?

Red-carpet welcomes. Not many couples have thought of them, but they're one of the building blocks for a great marriage.

They're creative. They're special. And they're just for you two.

21

Your Church Connection

A ship out at sea in fog and gloom became aware of a hulking shape ahead. It looked as if a collision was coming. . . .

Quickly the captain sent an order through the semi-darkness: "Alter your course 10 degrees north!"

Back came a message: "Alter *your* course 10 degrees south!"

The captain couldn't believe the impertinence. He sent a second message: "Alter *your* course 10 degrees north. I am the captain!"

A message came back: "Alter *your* course 10 degrees south. I am seaman third class."

The captain was furious; by now they were too close for comfort! He flashed back, "Alter your course 10 degrees north! *I am a battleship.*"

Back flashed the reply: "Alter your course 10 degrees south! *I am a lighthouse.*"

There's one issue in your married life you can't adjust, but you *simply have to adjust to it.* It's so basic, so right, so universally agreed on, there's no changing it. You two are the ship in the fog, and it's the lighthouse. What is it? Your strong connection together with a good local church.

Did you have separate churches before marriage? You may want to find a third, for neutral ground. It may not be either of your parents' churches, if you need to establish your own identity as a couple.

Even on your honeymoon, go to church. *You must love God before you love each other.*

If you don't know for a while what your permanent church is going to be, still attend somewhere every Sunday—but shop around. Only when the Lord has given you clear direction and you've both prayerfully agreed, will you want to join; it's so life-shaping and important!

Even after that, don't jump into heavy involvement until your first anniversary. Remember God's instructions to the people of Israel (Deuteronomy 24:5), and for one year specialize in adjusting to each other.

How will you find the right church for the two of you? Ask these nine questions of any church you're considering:

1. Does the church preach Christ?

2. Does it seem based on the Bible?

3. Do you each have an "inner witness" from the Lord that He wants you there?

4. Does it provide opportunities for you to grow?

5. Can you bring your non-Christian friends there?

6. Is there a missionary program?

7. Are the church leaders good models for living?

8. Are there opportunities for you to serve?

9. Is it close enough for you to get really involved?

When we say we love Jesus Christ, that means we love not only the Head but the Body; the two are mystically one. And though believing in Him makes you a member of the "Church universal," the invisible Church, still God calls you also to become part of the visible, flesh-and-blood church, with faces and names and personalities.

If you're past your first anniversary, make sure you've joined and truly given your hearts away to the local fellowship. It won't be perfect; well, neither are you. But get into an adult Bible class or teach in Sunday school, and use your gifts, and develop friendships, and expose yourselves to all that God will do for you in that place.

Get involved, together. Get into a small group. (See my book *Discipling One Another,* Word Books, 1979.)

And as you get to know people more deeply, don't be disappointed! Hospitals are out to banish sickness, but they're filled with sick people. Churches are out to banish sin, but they're filled with sinners.

In the same body you'll find a Barnabas, a real encourager (Acts 4:36,37); an Alexander, who does the pastor a lot of harm (2 Timothy 4:14); a Dorcas who does nothing but good (Acts 9:36); a carnal Demas (2 Timothy 4:10); two women who quarrel (Philippians 4:2), and many other women who work hard for the Lord (Romans 16:12). They were all in the first-century church, and they're still in the twentieth—the wheat and the tares together. Well, we're not called to pull weeds, we're called to be wheat.

So just jump in together, function, and love your church![34]

22

Jealousy, the Glue of a Great Marriage

Whoever said that jealousy is a bad word? The Lord tells us:

> Love the Lord your God with all your heart and with all your soul and with all your strength . . . serve him only . . . for the Lord your God . . . is a jealous God. . . .
>
> Deuteronomy 6:5,13,15

Of course too much jealousy can get messy; so can too much mother love and lots of other good things. But if jealousy is one of God's attributes, let's look at this definition: "An intense appreciation of something that is precious and legitimately possessed, and an intense determination to defend that precious thing and its possession."

Sociologists and psychologists are beginning to suspect that the roots of jealousy are biological, like territoriality.

God seems to have made us with a way-deep-down need to share belonging with another.

And He made us in His own image, and He is like that. God is the ultimate Model Lover, and through the generations He's used every means to accomplish His goal of mutual "belonging-ness": "... I will say to those called 'Not my people,' 'You are my people'; and they will say, 'You are my God'" (Hosea 2:23). His desire for this was so intense that it drove Him to Calvary.

> *Place me like a seal over your heart,* [He woos us],
> *like a seal over your arm;*
> *for love is as strong as death,*
> *its jealousy unyielding as the*
> *grave.*
> *It burns like a blazing fire,*
> *like a mighty flame.*
> *Many waters cannot quench love;*
> *rivers cannot wash it away.*
> *If one were to give*
> *all the wealth of his house for love,*
> *it would be utterly scorned.*
> SONG OF SONGS 8:6,7

Pray for more, not less, jealousy!—not for the immature kind that makes you do childish things, like "making him/her jealous," which usually backfires. But pray for a flame of love so unquenchable that nothing can destroy it.

The opposite of holy jealousy is indifference. It's not

caring who makes a pass at your spouse; it's being good-natured and understanding over extra little flirtations; it's tolerance when two couples get too bold, too close with each other, and the words and actions get risqué in the name of friendship; it's being broadminded about unfaithfulness. . . .

There gets too much space between you when there's not the strong bonding of the glue of jealousy ! Let your whole beings cry out against all of that, "No, no, no!"

There must be an invisible barrier around the two of you, holding you together, that no one else can ever invade. Over the years there will be secrets no one else will ever know, and jokes the two of you think hysterically funny that no one else will ever hear.

Now, if there have been other marriages before, it will take longer for memories to fade and your "marriedness" to be secured. But intensely desire that "two-ness"! Be jealous for it! Jealousy is your glue.

But what if your mate already seems to be playing around? What if you suspect something—or even know something?

This is when jealousy becomes its purest and best. Welcome even the pain of it; it means you'll go to any lengths to get your marriage restored.

Don't say or do anything hastily, but pray for these five gifts from God:

1. *Ask Him for perspective.* Envision your marriage ten years from now, solid and loving and secure, when all this is healed.

2. *Ask Him for a cool head,* not to exaggerate the situation or even to get overly inquisitive about it. You don't need to know details—ever.

3. *Ask Him for new love techniques:* ways to serve and lift your partner, to build his or her self-esteem, and to increase the comfort and the warmth between you.

4. *Ask Him for a closed mouth,* not to spill anything to friends or family. Maybe you should seek a counselor for professional services. But otherwise, let your jealousy cover and seal over and keep hidden his or her precious reputation.

5. *And ask the Lord for healing for your marriage.* "More things are wrought by prayer than this world dreams of."

This is the assurance we have in approaching God: that if we ask anything according to his will, he hears us. And if we know that he hears us—whatever we ask—we know that we have what we asked of him.

1 John 5:14,15

Do you think God wants you to have a great marriage? Then *ask Him for it.*

23
What It Means to Stay Close

A gal said she didn't know where her husband was every night. One night she stayed home—and there he was!

You say you want to be close—but at the same time a warning yellow light goes off in your head: how close can you get without being bugged?

Some married couples are so incompatible they give up on having any more than dinner together most evenings and lovemaking, and that's about it.

Our friend Diane was telling us yesterday about a couple like this. Last summer they were vacationing in Europe and traveling separately, but they'd agreed to join each other in a certain city. The wife checked in on schedule and had four days there before she happened to run into her husband downtown! They'd missed cues on what hotel—and Diane said neither one was bothered by it!

That's not a great marriage—and they have no idea of the glory of Genesis 2:23,24. I've quoted a little of it; let's get the whole thing:

> *And [Adam] said,*
> > *"This is now bone of my bones*
> > *and flesh of my flesh;*
> > *she shall be called 'woman,'*
> > *for she was taken out of man."*

> Therefore shall a man leave his father and his mother, and shall cleave unto his wife: and they shall be one flesh.

KJV

That verb *cleave* is unusual; it has two opposite meanings. It can mean to split apart, as a meat "cleaver," or else it means to join together. When it means the latter, as it does here in Genesis, the word is unbelievably strong. Dr. Ed Wheat says it means these things:

> To cling to or adhere to, abide fast, cleave fast together, follow close and hard after, be joined together, keep fast, overtake, pursue hard, stick to, take, catch by pursuit, . . . to cement together, to stick like glue—or be welded together so that the two cannot be separated without damage to both.[35]

This kind of intimacy—cleaving—sounds as if the ideal marriage would be for two lives to be perfectly superimposed on each other.

But what does cleaving mean, practically? If cleaving is God's strong command, if it's an essential building block to a great marriage, does it mean, ideally, you're to be together twenty-four hours a day?

Suppose some newlyweds go to a ball game. He thinks it great, but she's bored. How will they manage to cleave to each other? By forcing the husband to give up baseball for life? By forcing the wife to go whether she likes it or not? Either to go and hate it, or to stay home and sulk—neither one is cleaving.

Cleaving is not refusing to be apart. *Cleaving is constantly guarding each other's hearts, keeping each other as warm and happy and loving as possible.* And that's a building block to a great marriage.

So the wife will enthusiastically encourage her husband to go with the guys to the ball game, and the husband will not whine for her to come along. They are both glad to assure the other's happiness. That's staying intimate!

Ray and I are more intimate, we're cleaving more, this thirty-eighth year than ever before. Working together full-time in our Renewal Ministries now that our children are grown, we know where each other is almost every moment. But the fifteen days of each month, when we're in town and not traveling, we leave each other alone for hours at a time.

We go separately to our office so we can be independent of each other. He's on the beach maybe an hour of each day, running, surfing, and studying his books on the sand. California sun makes my skin break out in a rash; I work indoors. To feel good he must have food and exercise; to feel good I must not eat too much and get plenty of sleep. He's an athlete, I'm not. He's a morning person, I'm not. Television meets his need to relax; total quiet relaxes me.

So we've learned to let the other be different (it takes a long time), while "constantly guarding each other's hearts, keeping each other as warm and happy and loving as possible."

> *your freedom*
> *is always tied in with mine*
> *i can let you go free fully*
> *if I am being let go by you*
>
> *my freedom liberates you*
> *which liberates me*
> *which liberates you*
> *etc.*
> *etc.*
> *etc.*
>
> *it can be an upward*
> *or a downward spiral*
>
> *i can choose*
> *you can choose*
> *we can choose*[36]

Ray's and my alonenesses are not our great delight;
they just give us breathing room. Losing our lives in each
other, honoring and helping each other, working for and
sharing in each other's successes—oh, these are our delight!

So what happens when we come together? You'll think
we're goofy. As often as one of us enters our office complex, we'll first head straight for the other's office for a
kiss. If we meet at home, we hug. When we're dressing I
often tell him, "I have to have a kiss to give me strength
to put on this shoe," and he'll drop everything to oblige.
Sometimes alone in an elevator we'll fall into each other's
arms until the door opens; my favorite thing is to get him
totally pinned so when the door opens he's caught in
public still struggling. In a hotel or airport sometimes we
separate, then rush back to each other, pretending we're
old friends who haven't met for a long time. I mean, it
gets pretty sickening, don't you think? No two people
should get that excited over each other. Especially after
all those years. I mean, really.

But if true delight in each other appeals to you when
you've been married a long time, be careful to stay intimate. In other words, "guard each other's hearts, keeping
each as warm and happy and loving as possible."

Cleave.

All your life.

24

Having Babies . . .

Most of us become parents long before we have stopped being children.

Mignon McLaughlin

Scene: Around the dining table of some friends

Characters: RICK, GINA, RAY, ANNE

GINA One of our neighbors, Trish, is having a partial hysterectomy. She and Mike have been married seven years, spending their money on fun. They thought they could have children anytime, and now she's scared it's too late. When we were newlyweds we didn't have any money, and things like ski trips never occurred to us. . . . We just stayed home (*laughing*) doin' what comes naturally.

(*The things we four friends discuss, we try to analyze; that's our style. There's more talk about Trish and the pill and family planning.*)

163

RAY "Meism" is at the heart of so much. Maybe not with Trish and Mike—I don't know them. But it's easy to want to please self first and postpone getting pregnant. "Let's get the apartment furnished." "Oh-oh, we ought to start buying a home." "Let the good times roll. . . ." There are always reasons to put off having a family.

ANNE And yet it's easier to have babies when you've got the old couch and the old rug, than later when everything's new and wonderful and you don't want it spit up on.

GINA And healthwise, it's good to have your children younger.

ANNE Maybe birth-control measures should be thought of for spacing babies, not for postponing them. Maybe that should come after the first pregnancy, not before it.

RICK Our friends Marsha and Jon are each waiting for the other to get "mature." Marsha says, "Jon's just a little boy yet at heart. He's not ready to be a daddy." And Jon says, "Marsha's so immature! She's not ready to be a mother." But when are you ever mature? Adults of any age are part little boy and little girl. Anyway, the more "mature" you get, the more rigid you are and hard to adjust!

ANNE It's maturing to have babies. Whether you feel like it or not, you change diapers, you get up for those two o'clock feedings. It's good for us to be forced out of our self-centeredness and into inconveniencing ourselves.

GINA If you're old enough to get married, you're old enough to have children.

RICK Fear is part of the problem. I sold insurance to Tom

and Berta, and they're Christians, but they're afraid to
bring children into this nuclear world. They wonder if it's
fair to the kids.

ANNE But Christian children are part of the solution, not
part of the problem! They're what this world needs—
people who will "hold forth the Word of life."

RAY Isn't it true that decisions based on fear instead of
on faith are usually faulty decisions!

GINA How about this "zero population" philosophy?
"Look out, folks, because we're about to run out of food,
or water, or space, or coal, or you name it."

RAY We'd all go crazy, wouldn't we, unless we trusted
God's Word! No wonder it brings us peace. From the beginning His first instructions were to "be fruitful and increase in number and fill the earth and subdue it." We
can trust Him that His instructions are still good and that
He's going to take care of us as we obey. And we can trust
Him in His time, before the world goes totally bonkers, to
bring Christ's return and set things right.

RICK Right. And in the meantime, faith and obedience
say to feed the poor, reach out to the needy, and pray for
rulers who make decisions about war and peace—but it
doesn't say not to have kids!

ALL You got it, you got it!

RICK Isn't it wonderful to go back to the basics for an-
swers? Back to God Himself, back to "Priority One," as
you preach to us, Ray—back to faith and obedience and
the Lord Himself?

(*Leaning earnestly across the table.*) God has the an-
swers. You just can't beat that Bible!

25

... And Adjusting to Babies

People who say they sleep like a baby usually don't have one.

LEO J. BURKE

Here I am writing this book, and here you are reading it, and maybe you're expecting your first baby next week. (For the average couple, the prechildren stage of marriage lasts just over two years.) Both of you are feeling very physical, aren't you—aware of a huge abdomen and swollen breasts, extra trips in the night to the potty, and exciting doctor visits for last-minute news releases. "He" is antsy from the cessation of intercourse; "she" couldn't care less right now; and maybe both are practicing their parts for that momentous experience of birth.

So the occasion finally comes. . . .

Perhaps you have a C-section. . . .

Or maybe your labor lasts for hours. . . .

Or maybe you're like a new mother I heard about. She shared a hospital room with my friend June when June had hers. This gal was crying because she didn't quite make it and she had her baby in the elevator.

The nurse said, "Honey, don't feel embarrassed; it happens here all the time; it's no big deal. Why, last year a woman had her baby right on the main front steps of the hospital, with a hundred people looking on!"

"I know!" the gal sobbed. "That was me!"

However the crisis of birth occurs, several predictable stages follow.

Stage 1: *Euphoria.* You can't believe that new little life. It's got all its fingers and toes. How *tiny* it is! You talk about who it looks like. And maybe you get flowers and cards and get pampered for a little.

Stage 2: *Declension.* "The tumult and the shouting dies. . . ." Mother's home now, whether you were before or not. Why does he cry so much? Why is he hungry at 3:00 A.M. when he was just hungry at 1:00? How do you decide whether he's cold or hot? How and how much do you pick him up? You change endless diapers. You have the initial shock of washing out dirty ones in the toilet. Your clothes get spit up on. Life's a blur of feedings, changes, and cotton swabs. There are new smells around, both good and bad, and the new equipment isn't new any

more, and there's a part of the house—where the basket
or crib is—which must now be forever adjusted to.

Your separate and together schedules, before so predictable, now have to bend to baby's needs and wants.
You lose sleep; you're tired; you can't socialize much;
there's a lot more work; the house gets messier; and however you operate as a parent, you feel guilty that you're
not doing a better job.

Stage 3: *Stabilization.* Baby starts sleeping through the
night, more or less; he's beginning to do cute things and
develop his little personality; you're enjoying sex together
again; the outside world is applauding you; and even the
in-laws are waxing enthusiastic. You finally decide,

> *Two are better than one.* . . .
> *A cord of three strands is not quickly*
>   *broken.*
>
> Ecclesiastes 4:9,12

Now you have a new decision to make. Chances are,
before Baby came the wife worked at a job outside the
home. Should she go back? Maybe, and maybe not.

But ask some careful questions about it:

1. Will your working add pressure to your marriage?

2. Do you have enough time and energy for it—emotional, physical, mental, spiritual?

3. Which is the greatest need, your need together for money, your personal fulfillment, or your baby's need for his mother's presence? (Please read my book *Children Are Wet Cement,* Fleming H. Revell, 1982.)

4. Does your husband's job need you, instead? Pastors, government officials, some businessmen need their wives as helpers and/or hostesses, and a wife's first reason for being a wife is to *help him* (Genesis 2:18).

5. Do you both feel enthusiastic about it?

6. Is *God* saying yes? The Scriptures don't give a black-and-white statement here, but the Holy Spirit will certainly tell you. Listen to Him and obey Him.

But whether or not you have that new decision, you do have one new danger.

Howard and Charlotte Clinebell say, "The point at which many marriages jump the track is in *overinvesting in children and underinvesting in the marriage.*"[37]

I'm writing now in Brazil. (I do jump around, don't I! We're ministering to missionaries, and all these yellow tablets go everywhere I go.) I just stopped writing in my hotel room to go down to the coffee shop for lunch with Maria, the wife of one of the outstanding pastors of this wonderful land.

Maria's beautiful face seems unmarred by the fact that she has four young children—three of whom came along to the pastors' conference where I've been speaking.

"I gave them the choice," she said. "Of course I left the baby home, but I told the others they could come if they wouldn't expect to be too much with Papa, because he would be very busy."

"Has it been all right?" I asked. "Did they have a good time?"

"I think so," she said. "It wasn't easy for either my husband or me to juggle conference and children. Neither of us got much sleep, and the children had to play in the hotel room with the sitter a lot. But still, coming along they could play with their papa in little spaces of time, and they also got more of a picture of what he is doing than if they'd been left home."

"It was a good choice," I said. "It gave *you* freedom to come to the conference, too—and it's so important for you to be with your husband all you can. Of course, he's an intense person, carrying such a big burden of leadership so young, and he needs you nearby whenever possible.

"Then you can understand and share his life, both his burdens and his victories. And besides, if you're there he'll also play. He'll take breaks; he'll get relief from the tensions. If you're not there, he'll just keep driving."

"He's already had a little heart problem," she said. I looked at those soft, big, brown eyes looking into mine, and I loved her.

"Maria," I said, "let the children be with sitters sometimes. They won't die. Your husband needs you nearby.

And when the children see the two of you so close and strong in your love, it will help them more than if you'd been with them every minute."

"Overinvesting in children!" How often the first baby, especially, gets overinvested in! He's going to be the perfect child. We've read all the books, and we're going to be the perfect parents, and anyway, he's so unusual, he smiled when he was only two weeks old, and he's very advanced for his age, and we have a special responsibility because he's obviously a genius. . . .

Back off, Mom and Dad. Take good care of your baby, yes. Love the fact that your two-ness has blended into one fresh miracle-product. You're a circle of three. Enjoy your baby together, caring for him, and playing with him together as often as you can.

But now—enough of that. It's time to get a sitter and go have a date. You say it's too expensive?

> *If babysitters charge a lot*
> *For services they render,*
> *Call grandma in to mind the tot,*
> *For she's the legal tender.*[38]

M.M PARISH

26

Analyze Who You Are

You're moving along. You're getting used to sharing the same last name, living at the same address. Maybe now there are babies there, too. . . .

Your new roles are adjusting to your personalities, and your personalities are adjusting to your new roles. As married people, you're becoming different, now: partly old and partly new.

Who are you, these new days? It's time to analyze yourself, analyze your mate, and then *accept what you find on both scores.*

Husband, you may be becoming one of these four types, or a combination of several of them:

1. Nester

2. Jock

3. Saint

4. Tycoon

Wife, you're becoming one or several of these:

1. Earth Mother

2. Vamp

3. Madonna

4. Amazon

Lets take a look at them one by one.

1. *Nester.* He's a family man above all. Will sacrifice a raise or a better job to keep the home life secure. Takes an active hand in chores and parenting. Has structured his priorities to turn down even church jobs and feel righteous about it, to be with his family. May possibly try too hard, be overbearing in his home, and produce unhappiness and eventual rebellion.

2. *Jock.* Very aware of his maleness. Intensely interested in sports, whether by participation or observation. Probably jogs, at least in spurts. May be egocentric, unable to form deep personal relationships; perhaps a true male chauvinist, demeaning women. Probably takes pride in casual or even sloppy dress.

3. *Saint.* Most oriented to and motivated by spiritual concepts. Loves church life. His intense participation in and occupation with things spiritual may produce pharisaical pride and make him obnoxious, or he may be truly godly, admired, and helpful. Apt to have a feminine, soft, sensitive side which makes him relate well to women.

4. *Tycoon.* Gives his major interest and efforts to his working place in the world. Intensely interested in his counterparts, whether friends or competitors. Goal oriented; willing to sacrifice temporary discomforts or instabilities to stay upwardly mobile in his career. Probably aware of his looks, stays well groomed. May be self-centered; may be insensitive in dealing with colleagues. Within this mind-set he may be in business, in the arts, in the ministry, in teaching—in many fields.

Each of these male types has a female counterpart.

1. *Earth Mother.* Her home and family are the center of her life. Intensely interested in all things nutritional, medical, and psychological as they relate to the home and family, and considers it spiritual not to have an outside job. Maybe bakes her own bread. Tireless worker. May not care much about her looks. Loves family routine and regulations. A "hovering" mother.

2. *Vamp.* Not necessarily immoral, though she may be. Very aware, whether healthily or otherwise, of her body and her sexuality. May be egocentric. Loves clothes and shopping for them; delights in being feminine and dresses to accentuate her femininity. Truly enjoys male company; may also enjoy females. Behind the scenes may or may not be a great sex partner. ("I don't mind living in a man's world as long as I can be a woman in it"—MARILYN MONROE.)

3. *Madonna.* Above all else, thinks spiritually. May be bored with non-Christian conversation. Intensely in-

terested in the Bible, in doctrine and related life-style, and in the church scene and personalities. Possibly may overparticipate, to the neglect of other areas of life. May be uptight and self-righteous, or may be truly godly and a blessing to many.

4. *Amazon.* A performer, an achiever. May be intellectual. Probably has a career outside of the home; enjoys the concourse of the world; loves to travel. May or may not struggle with her very independent spirit; may even have a hard, competitive, "male" personality.

How do you see yourself? I can see that Ray and I both have some of all four types in us. Probably my greatest personal struggle is wanting to be mostly a Madonna and seeing a lot of Amazon pop up! Poor Ray! Wouldn't you think any man would prefer a combination Earth Mother and Vamp?

But *he accepts me*—and that's a powerful building block toward a great marriage.

So what do you think? Do you have yourselves figured out?

> *Accept one another, then, just as Christ accepted you. . . .*
>
> Romans 15:7

Fully receive the way God is making you and the way He is making your partner. *Live with what you've got.*

Wife, if you've discovered you're married to a Nester,

don't expect him to bring you home a million dollars but love the fact that he keeps the lawn mowed.

If he's a Jock, think of the money you're saving because of the clothes he likes to wear.

If he's a Saint, at least you'll know where he is most of the time.

And if he's a Tycoon, share his pride, share his dreams, and help him become all he longs to be. God's kind of wife *helps* her man (remember Genesis 2:18). She doesn't fight what he is.

Husband, if you got an Earth Mother—boy, you should stay healthy.

If you got a Vamp, enjoy the scenery.

If you got a Madonna, shelter her from distractions, and learn from her.

But she's an Amazon? Unconsciously that must have been what you wanted. And there she is, at your side.

> *Woman was taken out of man's side*
> *to suggest her equality with him;*
> *not out of his feet to imply inferiority,*
> *not out of his head to suggest superiority,*
> *But out of his side, suggesting companionship,*
> *under his arm, to be protected,*
> *and next to his heart to be loved.*

She's at your side, but don't let her threaten you. Don't sink to the level of competing with her. She is female; remember her right to be "respected as the weaker partner"; treat her tenderly, uphold her, and reassure her.

But don't let her sass you. Let Ray be your model; he's been wonderful at taming his Amazon. (Deep inside, I don't want to be too big for my britches; no woman does.) How has he done it? Through the years he's remained a gentleman—a truly "gentle man"—and he's conquered me with his love. He has a great line for me when I need it: "Anne, I love you too much to let you get away with that. . . ."

It melts me.

So here's the building block: as you get to know who you're really married to, *accept that person totally.* Your eyes are more open now; *by an act of your will, decide to love what you have.*

27

Looking Forward

People change and forget to tell each other.

LILLIAN HELLMAN[39]

Decide to love what you have—but what *do* you have? One minute you think you know, but you're both growing and changing. You're trying to "think two," to stay intimate. . . .

But one day you wake up to the fact that *your spouse is no longer the person you fell in love with and married.*

Then what?

It's at this dangerous point that many marriages begin to crack open and break apart. He has changed; she has changed. Suddenly that other person seems like a stranger! But in the meantime, So-and-so at work really understands you; it's amazing how compatible you are. . . .

This is the situation that's produced "successive polygamy" in our generation. You marry somebody for a while; you outgrow them, and you divorce and remarry a person who is now right for you; but you continue to change, so you divorce again and marry someone else who's compatible *now*. . . .

You can see that this system does have advantages, because it's true that *you are not the same person you were at your wedding:* you have changed, and so has your partner.

So I recommend that you *do* get married over and over—but always to the same person.

Do the two of you sense that you've changed quite a lot? Then it's *time to recommit yourself to the new person your partner has become.*

Plan when you will do it. Make it a special occasion. Look into each other's eyes, hold each other's hands, and say again, "I, Michael, take you, Julie. . . ."

And through your lifetime together, *recommit yourselves as often as is necessary,* with or without a minister, friends, flowers, cake—and a honeymoon!

Here are the essentials of a traditional ceremony, so you'll have it ready any time you want to go through it again.

(*Begin with this, if another is reading.*)

"Friends, we are gathered together in the sight of God [and in the presence of this congregation] to join again ＿＿＿ and ＿＿＿ in holy matrimony, which is instituted by God, regulated by His Commandments, blessed by our Lord Jesus Christ, and to be held in honor among all men. Let us therefore remember that God has established and sanctified marriage, for the welfare and happiness of mankind. Our Savior has declared that a man shall leave his father and mother and cleave unto his wife. By His apostles, He has instructed those who enter into this relation to cherish a mutual esteem and love; to bear with each other's infirmities and weaknesses; to comfort each other in sickness, trouble, and sorrow; in honesty and industry to provide for each other, and for their household in temporal things; to pray for and encourage each other in the things which pertain to God; and to live together as the heirs of the grace of life.

"It is therefore not to be entered on lightly and unadvisedly, but thoughtfully, reverently and in the fear of God, with due consideration for the reasons for which it was ordained, and the duties which it imposes."

(*Here may be a prayer.*)

"_____, will you continue to have _____ to be your wedded wife, to live with her after God's ordinance in the holy estate of marriage? Will you love her, honor and keep her, in sickness and in health, and faithfully keep yourself to her alone, as long as you both shall live?"

Husband: "I will."

"And _____, will you continue to have _____ to be your wedded husband, to live with him after God's ordinance in the holy estate of marriage? Will you love him, comfort him, honor and keep him in sickness and in health, and faithfully keep yourself to him alone, as long as you both shall live?"

Wife: "I will."

Husband's vow: "I, _____, will continue to keep you, _____, as my wedded wife; to have and to hold from this day forward, for better, for worse, for richer, for poorer, in sickness and in health, to love and to cherish, as long as we both shall live."

Wife's vow: "I, _____, will continue to keep you, _____, as my wedded husband; to have and to hold from this day forward, for better, for worse, for richer, for poorer, in sickness and in health, to love and to cherish and to obey, as long as we both shall live."

(*If you're putting the ring on her finger.*)

Husband: "This ring I give you again, in token and pledge of our constant faith and abiding love."

(*If the wife is also again giving his ring.*)

Wife: "With this ring I wed you again, in the name of the Father and the Son and the Holy Spirit.

"Whither you go, I will go; where you lodge, I will lodge; your people shall be my people, and your God, my God."

(*Here there may be another prayer, followed by a kiss—and some sort of celebration!*)

And this building block of continual recommitment through the years is the last one I suggest to build for you a great marriage.

How is your "house"? Let's review with a checklist of the building blocks, and you may want to reread together any chapters you feel may help to strengthen your marriage.

Is your house on the solid rock of trust in Jesus Christ, as the Savior of each of you individually and as the Lord of your life together? (chapter 2).

Husband, are you seeking to husband your wife? Wife, have you memorized Ephesians 5:33 in The Amplified Version, and are you aiming at obeying it daily? (chapter 3).

Are you agreed on your process of decision making? (chapter 5).

Are you working at "thinking two"? Can you give recent examples? (chapter 6).

Are you frequently thinking or asking out loud "the

big question"? Repeat it to make sure you know it. (chapter 7).

Do you know the five-step communication exercise? Have you tried it? (chapter 8).

Explain how God is your Model in the art of reconciliation. (chapter 9).

Are you faithful at your daily quiet times? (chapter 12).

Is your sex life improving? Do you both think so? (chapter 14).

Can you each name your partner's rights, and are you seeking to give them? (chapter 16).

Have you made goals together? Can you repeat them? For what future date? (chapter 17).

Have you made out a budget, and are you living by it? What did Wesley suggest you do with your money? (chapter 18).

How often are you with your parents and friends? Does it seem about right, too much, too little? (chapter 19).

If you're past your first anniversary, are you active in the church you've chosen? (chapter 21).

Can you define "staying close"? How would you rate yourselves at this point? (chapter 23).

If you don't have them already, are you planning to have children? (chapter 24).

Are you still in love? (chapter 26, 27). You are? Tell me about it. I'd like to know.

Sincerely yours,

32 Whitewater Drive
Corona del Mar, CA 92625

SOURCE NOTES

Chapter 1 You're Married!

1. Margaret N. Barnhouse, *That Man Barnhouse* (Wheaton, Illinois: Tyndale House Publishers, 1983), p.11.

Chapter 3 How to Act Like a Husband; How to Act Like a Wife

2. Robert O. Blood, *Marriage, Second Edition* (New York: The Free Press, 1969), page 202.
3. Paul Popenoe, *Marriage Before and After* (New York: Wilfred Funk, 1943), p. 191.
4. Blood, *Marriage, Second Edition,* p. 204.

Chapter 4 Responsibilities: Who Does What?

5. Robert O. Blood and Donald M. Wolfe, *Husbands and Wives* (New York: The Free Press, 1965), p. 107.

Chapter 5 The Decision-Making Process That Wins

6. Blood and Wolfe, *Husbands and Wives,* p. 357.

Chapter 6 Start to "Think Two"

6a. William Hill, "The Glory of Love" (New York: Shapiro, Bernstein & Co. Inc., 1936).

Chapter 8 Make Communication Your Favorite Indoor Sport

7. Ulrich Schaffer, *A Growing Love* (New York: Harper & Row, Publishers, Inc., 1977), p. 15.
8. Paul Tournier, *To Understand Each Other* (Richmond, Virginia: John Knox Press, 1967), p. 14.
9. Blood, *Marriage, Second Edition,* p. 121.
9a. Quoted by Howard and Charlotte Clinebell in *The Intimate Marriage* (New York: Harper & Row, Publishers, Inc., 1970), p. 256.

Chapter 9 Reconciliation: The Art of Making Up

9b. Quoted by Lawrence J. Peter in *Peter's Quotations* (New York: Bantam Books, 1977).
10. Quoted by Stuart Chase in "Vital Speeches of the Day," *Reader's Digest,* April, 1984, p. 153.
11. Elizabeth Achtemeier, *The Committed Marriage* (Philadelphia: Westminster Press, 1976), p. 171.
12. Quoted by Jack and Carole Mayhall, *Marriage Takes More Than Love* (Colorado Springs, Colorado: 1979), p. 56.
13. Ibid., p. 57.

Chapter 11 About Love

14. Larry and Nordis Christenson, *The Christian Couple* (Minneapolis: Bethany Fellowship, 1977), p. 34.

15. Roy Croft, *Leaves of Gold,* edited by Clyde Lytle (Williamsport, Pennsylvania: Coslett Publishing Company, 1938), p. 80.
16. Lois Wyse, *Love Poems for the Very Married* (New York: Harper & Row, Publishers, Inc., 1967), p. 41.

Chapter 12 Your First Together-Project

17. At any stationer's store, or write Renewal Ministries, 4500 Campus Drive, Suite 662, Newport Beach, CA 92660. Blue, black, or brown, or we'll send a brochure.
18. For more on these four principles, see my book *The Acts of Joanna* (Waco, Texas: Word, Inc., 1982).
19. *Seek* magazine, 8121 Hamilton Ave., Cincinnati, Ohio 45231.
20. *The Daily Walk* magazine, Walk Thru the Bible Ministries, Inc., P.O. Box 80587, Atlanta, GA 30366.

Chapter 13 Temple Gairdner's Prayer Before He Married

21. Quoted by David R. Mace, *Whom God Hath Joined* (Philadelphia: Westminster Press, 1953) p. 52.

Chapter 14 For Adults Only: Sex

22. Many quotations in this chapter are from Lawrence J. Peter, *Peter's Quotations* (New York: Bantam Books, 1977).
23. Clinebells,*The Intimate Marriage,* p. 136.
24. Wyse, *Love Poems for the Very Married,* p. 45.

Chapter 15 When You Can't Meet Each Other's Needs, Then What?

25. Achtemeier, *The Committed Marriage,* p. 119.
26. Bill and Gloria Gaither, "I Am Loved" (Nashville: The New Benson Company, 1978).

TAKE A BREAK: ET CETERAS ABOUT MARRIAGE

27. If your local stationer can't supply you, these can be ordered from Renewal Ministries, 4500 Campus Drive, Suite 662, Newport Beach, CA 92660
28. From *Spirit of Revival* magazine, Fall, 1983, published by Life Action Ministries, Buchanan, Michigan.

Chapter 16 Your Rights, Your Partner's Rights.

29. Popenoe, *Marriage Before and After,* p. 241.

Chapter 17 What Goals Do for You

30. Wayne Rickerson, *We Never Have Time for Just Us* (Glendale, California: Regal Books, 1982). From article adapted from this book entitled "Goal Setting in Marriage," which appeared in *Family Life Today* magazine, January, 1983, p. 25.

Chapter 18 Money: Make All You Can, Save All You Can, Give All You Can

31. Blood, *Marriage, Second Edition,* p. 234.
32. Ibid., p. 235.

Chapter 19 Outside Relationships: Delightful or Dangerous?

33. Genesis 2:24 KJV: "Therefore shall a man leave his father and his mother, and shall cleave unto his wife: and they shall be one flesh."

Chapter 21 Your Church Connection

34. Many of these thoughts were taken from a wonderful sermon by Dr. George Wood, pastor of the Newport Mesa Christian Center, Costa Mesa, California.

Chapter 23 What It Means to Stay Close

35. Dr. Ed Wheat, *Love Life for Every Married Couple* (Grand Rapids, Michigan: Zondervan, Inc., 1980), p. 30.
36. Schaffer, *A Growing Love,* p. 53.

Chapter 25 . . . And Adjusting to Babies

37. Clinebells, *The Intimate Marriage,* p. 236.
38. Quotes from *The Saturday Evening Post,* April 28, 1951.

Chapter 27 Looking Forward

39. Lillian Hellman, *Toys in the Attic* (New York: Random House).